THE AI PRODUCTION PLAYBOOK

Turning AI Experiments into Enterprise-Scale Business Systems

DORREN SCHMITT, PhD

The AI Production Playbook
Turning AI Experiments into Enterprise-Scale Business Systems
For CEOs, CFOs, and CIOs of SMBs

by Dorren Schmitt, PhD

Published by SkillBites LLC
www.skillbites.net

DISCLAIMER AND/OR LEGAL NOTICES

Internet addresses given in this book were accurate at the time it went to press.

Printed in the United States of America

For more information or to place bulk orders, contact the author or the publisher at info@skillbites.net

ISBN eBook: 978-1-952281-98-3
ISBN Paperback: 978-1-952281-96-9
ISBN Hardcover: 978-1-952281-97-6

Testimonials

"Every AI leader today is wrestling with the same problem: how to move from promising pilots to real, scalable impact. In *The AI Production Playbook*, Dorren Schmitt provides the missing structure—turning AI from isolated experimentation into a disciplined, enterprise capability.

As Head of Customer Experience, I'm in constant conversations about how AI can deliver meaningful results. What stands out most in Schmitt's approach is her unwavering focus on tying every initiative to measurable business outcomes. That principle—simple in theory, rare in practice—is what separates AI theater from true transformation.

This is more than an AI book. It's a practical guide for leaders who are ready to operationalize AI and make it work where it matters most: in the business."

—**Nick Kusko,** Head of CX, Opkalla, Charlotte, NC

"Most organizations treat governance as a speed bump, but Schmitt proves it is actually the accelerator. By embedding compliance and ethics into the very first gate of the innovation funnel, *The AI Production Playbook* shows how to avoid the 'compliance debt' that kills most projects before they scale. The MLOps-driven approach to continuous monitoring for drift and bias is the only way to build AI that customers and regulators can truly trust."

—**Miles Ward,** CTO, Insight, Seattle, WA

"Dorren Schmitt has the deep experience of providing technical leadership in high velocity teams. Her insight provides the ability to bridge business goals and execution."

—**Alex Theodore,** CTO, Edge Solutions, Alpharetta, GA

Dedication

In memory of my parents, who consistently encouraged the exploration of new ideas and endeavors. They instilled the curiosity that I have carried with me throughout my life.

Table of Contents

Author's Note

My 25-year tenure at The Weather Channel, with my current position as VP, IT Strategy & Innovation, has encompassed a period marked by profound technological transformations in both media and data science. Most notably, I spearheaded numerous efforts to establish the necessary infrastructure for providing hyper-localized, timely, and precise weather initiatives; navigated substantial evolution in computing technologies; and implemented the significant strategic adoption of cloud computing.

While these prior strategic and transformative projects served as invaluable learning experiences, the emergence of generative artificial intelligence (AI) presents a challenge and a fundamentally distinct opportunity. Generative AI is characterized by four unique attributes that necessitate a re-evaluation of the conventional principles governing project management and implementation upon which we previously relied: pervasive organizational impact, accelerated and constant evolution, deep data integration, and the launching of AI products. These compel us to transcend conventional digital transformation methodologies and to redefine the core principles essential for the successful deployment, scaling, and sustainment of AI products within the enterprise.

Over the past two-plus years, as I have disseminated my experiences through numerous conference presentations and panel discussions, a compelling narrative has become apparent: our organization has achieved a notable degree of success in moving AI products into production compared to many peer companies. Our approach is counterintuitive. We are achieving the launch of AI products by embedding the effort directly within our operational teams, rather than confining it within separate, dedicated innovation, architecture, or AI centers of excellence. Subsequent to several conference appearances, the consistent recommendation from numerous peers, who were impressed by our pragmatic success rate, served as the impetus for me to formalize these principles into a published work.

Reflecting upon the entirety of these discussions, presentations, and, most critically, tangible outcomes, I recognized that the foundation for our disproportionate success rests upon a framework of five essential pillars that constitute the structure of this book. While this framework is implementable by companies of any size, it is particularly significant for small to mid-size organizations that do not possess the extensive resources, dedicated innovation laboratories, or specialized architecture and AI teams characteristic of larger enterprises. I hope the approach discussed in this book enables SMBs to be successful in implementing AI in their organizations and welcome the opportunity to provide further assistance upon request.

CHAPTER 1

Architecting Your AI Strategy

The advent of artificial intelligence (AI) is orchestrating a profound transformation across industries, a shift so monumental it's often likened to the 19th-century Industrial Revolution. This contemporary evolution, frequently termed the "cognitive industrial revolution," promises an unprecedented surge in productivity. In 2025, analyses by firms such as McKinsey and Goldman Sachs projected the long-term economic impact of AI could range from $1 to $4 trillion in added productivity growth derived from diverse corporate use cases. This immense and clearly quantifiable potential serves as a powerful catalyst, compelling nearly all companies to substantially increase their investments in AI technologies and infrastructure over the coming years.

Despite this widespread and significant financial commitment to AI, the industry grapples with a considerable maturity gap. Extensive research consistently highlights a striking disparity: while almost every company is actively investing in AI, few leadership teams actually classify their organizations as "mature" within the AI deployment spectrum in 2025. Achieving true AI maturity signifies that AI is not merely an experimental technology but is deeply and seamlessly integrated into core business workflows, consistently and successfully driving substantial, measurable business outcomes. Consequently, the primary challenge is not in recognizing AI's transformative potential or in securing initial funding for pilot projects. Instead, it lies in effectively bridging the expansive chasm that separates nascent, experimental Proofs of Concept (POCs) from robust, scalable, and reliable production systems that deliver sustained value.

Further in-depth analysis reveals that the most significant imped-iment preventing companies from successfully scaling AI to a state of maturity is neither the inherent complexity of the technology itself nor a lack of technical talent, particularly in larger enterprises. Rather, it is fun-damentally attributed to a pronounced lack of focused, decisive direction and strategic guidance from senior leadership. This critical bottleneck is identified as primarily a *business challenge* rather than a purely techno-logical one. Addressing this necessitates a fundamental commitment from leaders to "rewire" their entire enterprises for change, actively disman-tling operational headwinds and bureaucratic inertia that invariably slow down execution. To effectively overcome this velocity barrier, the struggle to move from concept to widespread implementation, a comprehensive AI strategy must serve as the foundational blueprint for organizational restructuring, cross-functional alignment, and cultural transformation. It has been empirically observed that organizations with robust data and AI governance frameworks are strongly correlated with a remarkable 20–50% improvement in overall financial performance. Therefore, establishing effective governance mechanisms and ensuring clear strategic alignment from the project's inception is not merely a task of regulatory compliance or risk mitigation. Instead, it functions as the essential engine necessary for high-speed, de-risked value realization, directly counteracting the his-torical tendency of leadership failures to explicitly link robust governance structures with tangible, measurable financial outcomes. This integrated approach ensures that AI investments translate directly into sustainable competitive advantage and enhanced profitability.

Defining the AI North Star: Align Mission and Long-Term Vision

A successful AI strategy must function as the guiding "North Star," ensur-ing that every AI initiative, from the smallest POC to the largest pro-duction deployment, anchors firmly to the organization's core mission, objectives, and long-term vision. Strategy frameworks typically rely on multiple pillars: Vision & Business Alignment, Data Foundation & Governance, Technology & Infrastructure, Talent & Culture, and an Implementation Roadmap & Ethics.

Crucially, the organization must secure consensus from senior leaders on a strategy-led generative AI road map. This consensus-building step is challenging but critical for overcoming the operational headwinds that stall execution. The strategy must explicitly tie AI investments to maximizing profit, increasing market share, or achieving measurable operational resilience. The tangible outcomes, whether in increasing revenue, increasing speed to market, decreasing costs, and so on, are imperative. Without an explicit measurable impact, AI will be viewed as an isolated, experimental R&D budget item. AI must be a strategic tool for businesses seeking to thrive and must be leveraged to unlock new levels of success and efficiency. A successful AI strategy must function as the guiding "North Star," ensuring that every AI initiative, from the smallest POC to the largest production deployment, anchors firmly to the organization's core mission, objectives, and long-term vision. Without this clear strategic alignment, AI efforts risk becoming fragmented, inefficient, and ultimately unable to deliver tangible value. A robust AI strategy framework typically relies on multiple interdependent pillars, each critical for holistic and sustainable implementation:

- **Vision & Business Alignment:** This pillar establishes the overarching purpose of AI within the organization, directly linking AI initiatives to strategic business goals such as enhancing customer experience, optimizing operational efficiency, or driving innovation in new markets. It requires a clear articulation of how AI will contribute to competitive advantage and long-term growth.
- **Data Foundation & Governance:** Recognizing that AI models are only as good as the data they consume, this pillar focuses on establishing robust data acquisition, storage, quality, and management practices. It includes defining data ownership, ensuring data privacy and security, and implementing strong governance frameworks to maintain data integrity and compliance.
- **Technology & Infrastructure:** This pillar addresses the technical architecture required to support AI initiatives, encompassing

everything from computational resources and cloud platforms to AI development tools, MLOps (Machine Learning Operations) pipelines, and integration capabilities with existing systems. It involves selecting the right technologies to scale AI solutions effectively and securely.

- **Talent & Culture:** Building an AI-driven organization necessitates fostering a culture of innovation, continuous learning, and cross-functional collaboration. This pillar focuses on attracting, developing, and retaining AI talent (data scientists, ML engineers, AI ethicists), as well as upskilling the existing workforce to understand and leverage AI tools. It also involves promoting an ethical mindset in AI development and deployment.

- **Implementation Roadmap & Ethics:** This pillar outlines a phased approach for AI adoption, detailing specific projects, timelines, resource allocation, and success metrics. Crucially, it integrates ethical considerations from the outset, ensuring that AI systems are developed and deployed responsibly, fairly, transparently, and with accountability. This includes addressing potential biases, ensuring data privacy, and establishing mechanisms for human oversight.

Crucially, the organization must secure consensus from senior leaders on a strategy-led generative AI roadmap. This consensus-building step is not merely a formality but a challenging yet critical endeavor for overcoming the operational headwinds that frequently stall execution. Without executive buy-in, AI initiatives can easily become siloed, underfunded, and deprioritized. The strategy must explicitly tie AI investments to maximizing profit, increasing market share, or achieving measurable operational resilience. This involves clearly articulating the return on investment (ROI) and the strategic imperative of each AI project. AI must be recognized as a strategic tool for businesses seeking to thrive in an increasingly data-driven and competitive landscape, and it must be leveraged to unlock new levels of success and efficiency across all facets of an organization.

Value Stream I:
Empowering the Workforce

One of the most immediate and strategically critical value streams for AI deployment is the amplification of human potential, often termed Super-agency. This stream moves beyond simple automation, simply replicating inefficient human tasks. The focus becomes cognitive augmentation, utilizing AI to amplify human creativity, productivity, and positive impact. AI-powered software can adapt, plan, guide, and even assist in making decisions, significantly lowering the skill barriers required for employees to acquire proficiency in more domains.

Within this framework, AI-powered software acts as an intelligent co-pilot, designed to adapt to individual user needs, dynamically plan complex workflows, provide insightful guidance, and even assist in critical decision-making processes. This profound integration of AI significantly lowers the skill barriers traditionally required for employees to acquire proficiency in more fields. By democratizing access to advanced cognitive support, Superagency empowers individuals to tackle more sophisticated challenges, learn new skills with greater ease, and ultimately contribute at a higher level than previously possible, transforming the nature of work and innovation.

Focusing on employee empowerment provides the necessary short-term returns to justify the massive long-term investment opportunity. These initiatives generate quick, measurable return on investment (ROI) by applying practical applications of AI in daily work.[1] For instance, enterprises are transforming Human Resources (HR) by using AI and automation to cut internal support ticket volumes, streamline onboarding processes, and deliver faster, more personalized employee support. This operational win directly translates to freeing HR professionals to focus on strategic work, which, in turn, fuels engagement, retention, and overall company culture. By delivering immediate, measurable ROI through employee-focused AI, organizations strategically de-risk the overall AI portfolio, providing tangible success stories to a potentially skeptical leadership team.

Value Stream II:
Bringing New Products to Market

AI should be systematically employed to accelerate the entire product lifecycle, from initial ideation and prototyping through to Minimum Viable Product (MVP) launch. The fundamental approach must still be human-centered, involving a deep understanding of customer problems, empathy for the end-user, and the maintenance of a continuous feedback loop.

AI technology significantly accelerates the development process itself. Tools can automatically generate code snippets and simplify machine learning model development for predictive features in MVPs, such as the capabilities offered by platforms like Google's AutoML. Key best practices for this value stream include defining clear, measurable objectives for the AI feature, ensuring the quality of the data is paramount, and establishing an AI ethics committee to address potential ethical concerns, such as bias, before launch.

Value Stream III:
Enhancing Existing Products with
AI Features

For existing product lines, AI serves as a mechanism for continuous competitive advantage through deep integration, optimization, and personalization. This involves leveraging AI to uncover patterns in user behavior and enable data-driven decision-making post-launch.

A classic example of this is the constant optimization of recommendation engines, such as those used by Amazon, which utilize advanced algorithms based on customer behavior to significantly increase sales and personalization. This strategy mandates continuous performance monitoring of AI features and subsequent improvements based on user feedback and analytical data. Crucially, all AI enhancement initiatives must align with broader business goals, ensuring they contribute measurably to the product's success metrics, such as increasing conversion rates or improving customer lifetime value.

Value Stream IV:
Automating Processes and Efficiency

The most foundational strategic objective for AI often centers on driving core efficiency gains and cost reduction through the automation of operational processes. AI-driven automation capabilities span a wide range of business functions, including inventory management, logistics, accounting, customer service, and routine data entry.

Do not fall into the trap of automating flawed tasks/processes. Workflows should be evaluated during development to gain efficiencies that automation can provide. But by automating repetitive and time-consuming tasks, AI facilitates improved operational efficiency. The resulting strategic outcome is not simply cost savings but the reallocation of valuable human capital. When routine tasks are handled by AI, employees are freed to dedicate their time to more complex, creative, and high-value strategic work, thereby optimizing the organization's overall intellectual and operational output.

Value Stream V:
Risk Management, Decision Intelligence, and Sustainable Growth

A mature AI strategy recognizes that the technology's role extends beyond efficiency and consumer interaction to serve as a critical tool for enterprise resilience, sustainable growth, and improved strategic decision-making.

Improved Decision Intelligence: AI excels at analyzing large volumes of data in real time, yielding valuable insights for informed decision-making. This capability is especially powerful in areas like marketing, sales, and research, where data analysis identifies trends and consumer behavior patterns, allowing companies to adapt their strategies more effectively.

Real-Time Risk Management: Machine Learning has been used for a couple of decades to analyze patterns and irregularities in data in real time to identify potential risks, such as emergent cyber-attacks. This has exploded with Generative AI. This capability allows businesses to significantly reduce the time between threat detection and response, establishing superior operational resilience. This sophisticated use of AI demands that governance be continuously embedded and operationalized, especially in risk-sensitive sectors like finance, healthcare, and defense. Responsible AI adoption requires clear standards for auditability, explainability, and bias mitigation to ensure these decision systems remain trustworthy.

Framework for Strategic Portfolio Planning

The successful execution of an enterprise-wide artificial intelligence (AI) strategy hinges on the critical translation of the high-level architectural blueprint into a rigorous, measurable portfolio plan. This is not a passive administrative task; it is a foundational strategic necessity that links technical ambition directly to financial and operational accountability in quantifiable business outcomes. This principle ensures that every AI investment, from initial exploration to full-scale deployment, is fundamentally justified by a clear, pre-defined, and measurable path to achieving a positive production.

This structured approach injects essential financial and operational rigor into the entire AI investment lifecycle, transforming the development process from a series of isolated technical experiments into a disciplined, value-driven portfolio management system. The approach demands clear metrics, staged gates for progression from POC to production, and a governance model focused squarely on measurable business impact. In essence, this portfolio framework transforms the AI strategy from a conceptual vision into an auditable, financially responsible operational plan, ensuring every dollar spent contributes directly to the organization's strategic and financial goals.

AI Strategy Matrix: Value Streams and Success Metrics

Strategic Objective	Primary Business Goal	Key Performance Indicator (KPI)	Risk Mitigation Focus
Empowering Employees (Superagency)	Productivity & talent retention	Increase in employee productivity score (EPS), decrease in internal support ticket volume	Bias in resource allocation, data privacy
New Product Development	Market penetration/ revenue growth	Time-to-market reduction, new revenue % from AI products, increase in accuracy	Model reliability, intellectual property, and introduction of vulnerabilities
Operational Automation	Cost reduction & efficiency	Reduction in operating cost per unit, time saved on routine tasks	Process drift, explainability gaps
Decision Intelligence	Competitive advantage & resilience	Improvement in forecast accuracy, reduction in incident detection time, data-driven decisions	Data quality, hallucinations, security compliance, data privacy

CHAPTER 2

The Five Operational Pillars for Production Success

The achievement of a high project success rate in moving AI from a technical Proof of Concept to a trusted, scalable production system relies entirely upon the institutionalization of five core operational pillars. A successful POC merely demonstrates technical feasibility; a successful production launch requires enterprise-grade trust, compliance, and sustained value delivery. These pillars formalize the non-negotiable requirements related to Governance, Data/Technology, and Talent/Culture, ensuring that the organization is ready to capture the strategic value streams defined in chapter 1.

Pillar One: Data Readiness— The Foundation of AI Success

The fundamental pillar of AI production success is data. Organizations must have a comprehensive grasp of what data they possess, where it resides, and who maintains access and ownership. Failure to establish robust data management and governance *before* large-scale AI deployment leads to project delays, underperformance, and severely inflated costs, as data strategies must be retrofitted later. But don't be paralyzed. This is where many companies are failing. As with many other technology foundations, data management, governance, ownership, and security are never-ending.

Forward-thinking organizations treat data as a product. It is a reusable asset that supports multiple outcomes over time, rather than a resource tied only to a single project, operation, or team. Many data sources are reusable to support a multitude of outcomes.

To effectively implement and reinforce this product-centric approach, organizations must meticulously catalog all key data flows. This catalog should be comprehensive, detailing the following critical attributes for each data stream:

- **Source System:** Identifying the origin of the data is crucial for understanding its lineage, potential biases, and the initial point of data quality control.
- **Refresh Rate:** Documenting how frequently the data is updated provides insights into its currency and suitability for various use cases, particularly real-time or near-real-time applications.
- **Sensitivity Level:** Classifying data by its sensitivity (e.g., public, internal, confidential, restricted, personally identifiable information [PII], protected health information [PHI]) is paramount for ensuring compliance with privacy regulations (like GDPR or CCPA) and implementing appropriate security measures.
- **Downstream Users and Applications:** Understanding who consumes the data and for what purposes reveals its impact across the organization and helps in prioritizing data quality initiatives.
- **Impact of Disruption:** A critical yet often overlooked aspect is to assess and document the potential business impact should the data flow be interrupted or cease entirely. This includes financial implications, operational disruptions, and risks to decision-making or compliance.

Beyond merely Cataloging, establishing clear ownership is imperative. A dedicated **data owner** must be assigned for each high-value dataset. This individual or team is responsible for the overall health, integrity, and life-cycle of the data product. To further delineate responsibilities and ensure explicit accountability for data quality, access control, and other critical aspects, a **RACI** (Responsible, Accountable, Consulted, Informed) **table** should be defined. This framework clarifies who is:

- **Responsible:** individual(s) who do the work to achieve the task
- **Accountable:** the individual ultimately answerable for the correct and thorough completion of the deliverable or task, ensuring its quality and timeliness
- **Consulted:** individual(s) whose opinions are sought, typically subject matter experts
- **Informed:** individual(s) who are kept up-to-date on progress or decisions

Finally, to truly validate and demonstrate the value delivered by these meticulously managed data assets, their contribution must be rigorously tracked and measured. This requires establishing clear metrics directly tied to overarching business outcomes. Examples of such metrics include:

- **Added Revenue:** quantifying how data insights directly lead to new sales, customer acquisition, or expanded market share
- **Increase in Model Accuracy:** demonstrating how high-quality data improves the predictive power and reliability of analytical models, leading to better forecasts or more effective automated processes
- **Operational Efficiency Gains:** measuring reductions in costs, processing times, or error rates achieved through data-driven optimizations
- **Improved Customer Satisfaction:** tracking how personalized experiences or enhanced services, enabled by data, positively impact customer loyalty and feedback

By adopting this holistic framework, an organization ensures that its data product strategy contributes measurably and strategically to the enterprise's success, transforming raw data into a powerful engine for innovation and competitive advantage.

The vast majority of organizational data, approximately 80%, exists in unstructured forms. This includes a wide array of sources, such as emails, chat messages, call recordings, documents, videos, and various other media types. Within this unstructured data lies a rich and largely untapped reservoir of contextual, unfiltered insights that are critical for informed decision-making and advanced analytical applications.

To effectively unlock and leverage this immense value, organizations must establish a robust data infrastructure. A foundational requirement is the implementation of shared storage with strong data governance. This storage system must be capable of accommodating not only traditional structured files but also raw media in its native format. Critically, this storage infrastructure needs to be equipped with search layers. These search capabilities should encompass full-text search for comprehensive keyword-based retrieval and, crucially, vector search. In today's world, much of this data sits in on-prem file shares, Microsoft SharePoint, Google Docs, and other SaaS products. Being able to tap into a variety of file locations improves the value of your data and provides more robust data-driven decisions.

Beyond mere storage, a significant emphasis must be placed on automating the capture and enrichment of this data. This involves setting up well-defined data pipelines that can automatically process and enhance the raw input. Key automated processes within these pipelines include:

- **Transcription:** Automatically converting audio and video recordings into searchable text.
- **Entity Extraction:** Utilizing Large Language Models (LLMs) to identify and extract key entities, such as names, dates, locations, and specific terms, from textual data.
- **Text Embedding Generation:** Converting extracted text into high-dimensional vector embeddings, which capture the semantic meaning of the text. These embeddings are then stored in a specialized vector index for fast and efficient similarity searches.
- **Meta-Data:** Having tags in documents, video, audio recordings, etc., that provide rich context adds to the usability of the content.

Finally, to truly maximize the utility of both structured and unstructured data, it is imperative to integrate these disparate data sources. This integration should be achieved by "wiring together" the data using shared identifiers. Examples of such identifiers include a universal customer ID, product ID, or transaction ID. By establishing a common linkage through these identifiers, organizations can create a unified schema. This unified schema provides a holistic and consistent view of all organizational data, enabling reliable and comprehensive AI querying across all data types, thereby empowering more accurate and insightful AI applications.

Before committing substantial resources to a POC, the organization must prevent resource misallocation and project failure by objectively measuring its AI maturity level against its current capabilities and data assets.

Organizations must evaluate their skills, data availability, and infrastructure to establish a realistic foundation for adoption. Projects frequently fail when organizations attempt implementations that exceed their technical maturity or data readiness.

AI Maturity Level Assessment Framework

AI Maturity Level	Skills Required	Data Readiness Profile	Feasible AI Use Cases
Level 1 (Basic Adoption)	Basic understanding of AI concepts. Ability to integrate data sources and map out prompts.	Minimal to zero unique data available. Enterprise data available.	Quickstart projects. Any Copilot, Gemini, or OpenAI solution.
Level 2 (Custom Analytical)	Experience with AI model selection and deployment. Familiarity with data cleaning/ processing.	Small, structured dataset. Small amount of domain-specific data available.	Custom analytical AI workload. Custom generative AI chat app (no RAG). Automated ML training, VertexAI for specific automation.
Level 3 (Production Scaling)	Deep MLOps expertise. Advanced Data Engineering for data fabric. Cross-functional Governance/ Ethics expertise.	High-quality proprietary data. Contextual/ unstructured data indexed. Synthetic data pipelines established.	Full-scale RAG applications. Multi-agent systems. Mission-critical predictive models.

Pillar Two: Educating Associates— Building AI Fluency and Trust

Successful scaling is heavily dependent on the willingness and ability of the workforce to adopt new AI tools and workflows. Establishing organizational AI literacy builds a culture that is receptive to change and accelerates adoption speed.

To successfully integrate AI within any organization, a foundational cultural shift is paramount. Leaders must consistently articulate and demonstrate that AI serves to **augment, not replace**, human capabilities. This framing is not merely a semantic choice; it's a strategic imperative that directly addresses common employee anxieties and resistance to new technologies. By positioning AI as a tool that enhances productivity, streamlines workflows, and frees up human talent for more complex and creative tasks, organizations can transform skepticism into active engagement. This cultural bedrock is crucial for fostering an environment where employees view AI as an ally rather than a threat, ultimately facilitating smoother adoption and greater overall success.

Beyond cultural messaging, comprehensive and strategically designed training programs are indispensable. Generic, one-size-fits-all education will prove insufficient for meaningful AI adoption. Instead, training must be robust, targeted, and highly practical. This necessitates the development and deployment of hands-on workshops and digital courses that are specifically tailored to the diverse roles and responsibilities within the organization. For instance, data scientists will require in-depth technical training on AI model development and deployment, legal teams will need to understand the ethical and compliance implications of AI, sales and HR personnel can benefit from AI-powered tools for customer relationship management and talent acquisition, and finance departments can leverage AI for predictive analytics and fraud detection. By customizing training to the specific needs of each department and role, employees can immediately grasp the practical relevance and value of AI in their daily tasks, thereby accelerating the integration phase and effectively mitigating potential adoption resistance.

Furthermore, given the unprecedented pace of AI's evolution, continuous learning must be ingrained into the organizational culture. This can be achieved through a multifaceted approach that includes internal mentorship programs, where experienced AI practitioners can guide and support their colleagues. Online, on-demand extended learning materials, such as curated courses and knowledge bases, provide flexible access to new information and skills. Knowledge-sharing initiatives, like internal forums, communities of practice, and regular seminars, further foster a collaborative learning environment. The economic significance of AI literacy has been widely recognized, with governmental bodies such as the US Department of Labor actively encouraging the use of grants and funding streams to bolster AI training across the workforce. This external recognition underscores the critical importance of investing in corporate AI literacy as the essential onramp to successful production adoption. By demonstrating immediate, practical value through targeted and continuous training, organizations can not only address and eliminate adoption resistance but also unlock the full transformative potential of AI.

Pillar Three: Establishing an Innovation Committee

Governance serves as the indispensable structural framework that underpins the safety, accountability, and strategic coherence of an organization's entire AI portfolio. It represents the critical shift from viewing AI systems as unregulated experiments to integrating them as trusted, operational components within the enterprise. Crucially, governance must be intrinsically embedded into the foundational design and development stages of AI, ensuring that robust risk management practices evolve dynamically alongside advancements in technological capabilities. This proactive and integrated approach is paramount for fostering sustainable and ethical AI innovation.

To effectively implement and oversee this crucial governance framework, the establishment of a dedicated **Innovation Committee** is a non-negotiable requirement. This committee must be endowed with a clear and comprehensive mandate: to establish, enforce, and continually refine clear standards across several key dimensions, including:

- **Explainability:** ensuring that the decision-making processes of AI systems are transparent and understandable to human users and stakeholders
- **Auditability:** establishing mechanisms for systematically reviewing and verifying the performance, data inputs, and outputs of AI systems
- **Bias Mitigation:** actively identifying, assessing, and implementing strategies to reduce or eliminate unfair biases that could lead to discriminatory or inaccurate outcomes

The efficacy of this committee hinges on its cross-functional composition. It must draw together key decision-makers and subject matter experts from a diverse range of departments, including:

- **Legal:** to ensure compliance with existing and emerging regulations
- **Security:** to safeguard against cyber threats and data breaches
- **IT:** to manage the infrastructure and technical integration of AI systems
- **Data Ownership:** to ensure proper data provenance, privacy, and ethical use
- **Human Resources:** to address the impact of AI on workforce dynamics and ethical employment practices
- **Finance:** to evaluate the economic viability and return on investment of AI initiatives
- **Sales and Marketing:** to understand customer impact and ethical communication of AI capabilities
- **Product Leadership:** to guide the strategic development and responsible deployment of AI-powered products and services

This multi-disciplinary committee acts as the strategic gatekeeper for all proposed AI initiatives. It is responsible for rigorously reviewing all Proofs of Concept (POCs) against a formalized and comprehensive risk register. This register extends beyond mere technical feasibility, delving deeply into potential ethical concerns, such as the risk of generating false content (hallucinations) or the presence of embedded biases that could lead to unintended and harmful consequences.

A non-negotiable requirement for successful AI implementation is the incorporation of compliance and regulatory requirements from the very outset of the AI lifecycle, specifically during the POC phase. AI systems must be meticulously designed with regulatory demands in mind rather than attempting to retrofit compliance post-development. This proactive approach is crucial for preventing major legal and ethical complications that inevitably delay or, in many cases, completely derail production deployment.

This foresight prevents the accumulation of "compliance debt"—the massive and often prohibitive expense required to retroactively redesign, re-engineer, and validate models and data pipelines to meet regulatory standards later in the development cycle. By embedding compliance from the start, organizations significantly boost the long-term financial viability and operational efficiency of their AI production systems.

Furthermore, governance in AI is not a one-time event; it must be continuous. This means that robust oversight mechanisms are embedded into daily workflows and operational processes. Continuous governance necessitates the establishment of clear escalation protocols for identifying and addressing issues promptly, along with real-time monitoring capabilities. These measures ensure that all AI outputs are not only traceable back to their origins but are also defensible in terms of their ethical implications, accuracy, and adherence to established standards and regulations. This ongoing vigilance is essential for maintaining trust, ensuring accountability, and adapting to the evolving landscape of AI technology and its associated risks.

Pillar Four: Strategic Alignment—Tying Approved POCs to Business Outcomes

This foundational pillar is paramount for ensuring that an organization's valuable capital, resources, and burgeoning momentum are meticulously directed toward AI projects that genuinely advance strategic objectives. It mandates a rigorous pre-production commitment, demanding a demonstrable and measurable return on investment before any project transitions into full-scale production. Fundamentally, every approved POC must be explicitly and unequivocally linked to the overarching company strategy, its defined goals, specific objectives, or core mission. This intrinsic connection serves as a crucial filter, preventing the proliferation of projects that, while technically intriguing, fail to contribute meaningfully to the organization's strategic direction.

To operationalize this strategic alignment, the establishment of a robust POC-to-Key Performance Indicator framework is indispensable. This framework necessitates a shift in performance evaluation beyond conventional technical metrics such as model accuracy, precision, or recall. While these technical measures are important for assessing the internal quality of an AI model, they often do not fully capture the impact on the business. Instead, the evaluation must critically incorporate a broader spectrum of "business trust dimensions." These include, but are not limited to, **Fairness, Robustness, and Explainability (FRE):**

- **Fairness:** Ensures that AI systems do not perpetuate or amplify existing societal biases, treating all user groups equitably and avoiding discriminatory outcomes. This involves proactive identification and mitigation of bias in data and algorithms.
- **Robustness:** Guarantees that AI models perform consistently and reliably even when exposed to unexpected or adversarial inputs, ensuring their stability and resilience in real-world scenarios. This protects against vulnerabilities and maintains operational integrity.
- **Explainability:** Demands that the decision-making process of AI models is transparent and understandable to human stakeholders, fostering trust and enabling effective troubleshooting, auditing, and compliance. This moves AI from a "black box" to a more transparent and accountable system.

These non-technical metrics are not merely aspirational; they are absolutely critical for cultivating and securing enduring business trust, ensuring adherence to increasingly stringent regulatory compliance standards, and fostering sustained user adoption across the organization. Without a strong emphasis on FRE, even technically superior AI solutions risk rejection due to lack of trust or regulatory hurdles, ultimately hindering their ability to deliver value.

Compelling financial analysis consistently demonstrates a significant correlation between mature data and AI governance frameworks and improved financial performance. Organizations that actively prioritize and implement such frameworks, which inherently enforce the strategic alignment discussed, experience a substantial uplift in financial outcomes. This improvement often ranges between a remarkable 21% and 49%, indicating that robust governance and meticulous strategic alignment are not merely best practices but direct catalysts for financial success and competitive advantage. This data unequivocally validates that an investment in these foundational principles yields tangible and substantial returns.

Maintaining this critical alignment throughout the entire AI lifecycle necessitates early and continuous engagement with business stakeholders. This proactive and iterative approach fosters a continuous feedback loop, ensuring that AI use cases remain firmly tethered to real-world applications and are constantly refined and optimized through the pilot and subsequent scaling phases. This iterative refinement prevents the development of solutions in a vacuum, ensuring they meet evolving business needs.

Furthermore, the Innovation Committee plays a pivotal role in enforcing this strategic discipline. It must actively exercise its authority to deny production funding to projects that fail to establish and meet the stipulated FRE metrics and demonstrably achieve their defined ROI goals. This stringent oversight is crucial for preventing the misallocation of precious organizational resources into underperforming or strategically misaligned projects. By upholding these standards, the Innovation Committee reinforces the strategic imperative, ensuring that only value-generating AI initiatives progress to full-scale implementation, thereby safeguarding financial health and strategic focus.

Pillar Five: Annually Funding the POC Pipeline with a Dedicated Budget

The journey from isolated Proof-of-Concept triumphs to a consistently reliable AI production pipeline demands a fundamental shift in organizational funding strategies. To truly unlock the transformative potential of artificial intelligence, organizations must commit to predictable, sustained financial investment, specifically ring-fenced for the critical POC pipeline. This dedicated budget must be carefully insulated from the typical pressures and short-term demands of operational expenditures (OpEx). Crucially, this financial commitment needs to be explicitly and unequivocally tied to the organization's overarching growth-oriented strategic mission, ensuring that AI initiatives are always aligned with the highest-level business objectives.

The broader investment landscape provides a robust and compelling justification for this dedicated funding approach. Global investment in AI is experiencing an unprecedented surge, reflecting the widespread recognition of its strategic importance. Capital expenditures in AI are exploding, with the rapidly evolving field of generative AI alone anticipated to witness an exponential growth in investment in the future. This substantial influx of capital underscores a global commitment to harnessing AI's capabilities.

However, with increased capital expenditure comes the imperative for organizations to rigorously justify these investments by demonstrating a high potential for ROI. Industry leaders consistently report a threefold higher ROI over a three-year period for companies that make significant AI investments compared to those with minimal engagement. Achieving this necessitates a strategic internal reallocation of resources. Funds must be purposefully diverted from what might be considered "mature areas of the budget," those established, often lower-growth areas, and prioritize high-potential AI initiatives that promise to drive future growth and competitive advantage. This strategic reallocation is not merely a cost-cutting measure but a deliberate act of investing in the future.

The dedicated POC budget should be conceptualized and managed using a Corporate Venture Capital (CVC) approach. This sophisticated model recognizes that AI innovation, particularly at the POC stage, carries inherent risks but also offers extraordinary rewards. High-coherence strategies are essential here, effectively bridging economic competitiveness objectives with robust and flexible innovation funding instruments.

Under this CVC framework, capital tranches are not released in a single lump sum but are contingent upon the successful navigation of clearly defined strategic checkpoints. These checkpoints, established and rigorously monitored by an empowered Innovation Committee (Pillar 3 of the overall AI strategy framework), ensure that each POC progresses with purpose and alignment. Furthermore, the release of subsequent tranches is tied to the consistent achievement of measurable KPIs (Pillar 4). These KPIs provide objective evidence of progress, impact, and continued viability.

The consistent and predictable allocation of this dedicated fund serves as the clearest and most measurable signal of leadership's profound commitment to "steering fast enough" and adapting quickly to technological advancements and market shifts while capitalizing effectively on successful POCs. Without this critical mechanism, the often-arduous transition from POC feasibility demonstration to full-scale production deployment becomes inevitably stalled. Such delays are almost always a direct consequence of capitalization issues, where promising initiatives lose momentum due to a lack of consistent, accessible funding, ultimately hindering the organization's ability to fully realize its AI ambitions.

The Roadmap to Trusted, Scaled AI

The successful leap from POC to enterprise production is a structured, managed transition requiring the operationalization of the five pillars—Data Readiness, Workforce Education, Governance, Strategic Alignment, and Dedicated Funding. This transition must be managed through clear phases, moving from conceptual feasibility to validated business value and full regulatory compliance.

AI Data Readiness Roadmap: Transitioning from POC to Production

Phase	Time Frame (Est.)	Core Data & Governance Activities	Pillars	Success Metric
Proof of Concept (POC)	4-8 weeks	Define Minimal Viable Dataset (MVD). Secure data owner approval [P1]. Incorporate Compliance and Governance requirements from the start [P3]. Engage business stakeholders early [P4].	P1, P3, P4	Technical feasibility demonstrated. MVD approved. Compliance framework defined.
Pilot	8-12 weeks	Catalog full set of production data. Automate data quality checks [P1]. Implement Targeted Training for core users [P2]. Implement initial Human-in-the-Loop (HITL) system.	P1, P2, P3, P5	Measurable ROI demonstrated on pilot use case [P4]. Trust established. Initial funding tranche justified [P5].
Scale to Production	6-12 months	Build Connected Data Fabric/Semantic Layer for 3-5 domains [P1]. Establish Synthetic Data pipeline [P1]. Implement continuous governance (FRE monitoring) [P3]. Release funding tranches based on KPI adherence [P5].	P1, P3, P5	Full regulatory compliance achieved. Organizational readiness for 10+ AI use cases. Revenue target reached.

The remainder of this comprehensive guide delves into each of the five foundational pillars, offering actionable insights and practical methodologies for their successful execution. It is crucial to understand that each pillar represents a distinct journey of maturity rather than a fixed state to be achieved instantaneously. While complete maturity in every pillar is not a prerequisite for successfully transitioning POCs into full-scale production, initiating these journeys and establishing a solid foundational framework are essential. By embarking on these individual maturation processes, organizations can progressively build the capabilities and infrastructure necessary to support robust, scalable, and effective AI solutions. This iterative approach ensures that progress can be made incrementally, allowing for continuous improvement and adaptation as the organization's AI strategy evolves.

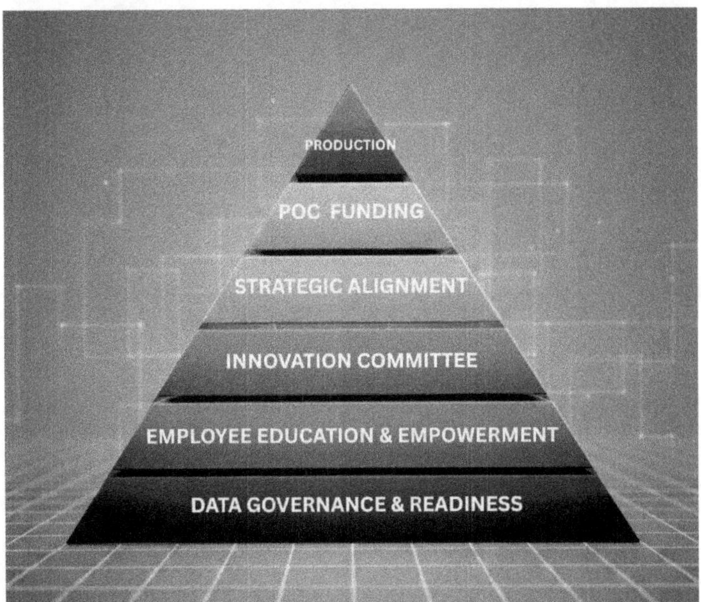

The pyramid structure illustrates a strategic roadmap where **Production**—the successful, large-scale deployment and operation of AI solutions—is the ultimate pinnacle, achievable only by diligently building the first five foundational steps. The base, **Data Governance and Readiness**, ensures data quality and accessibility; this is followed by **Associate Education and Empowerment**, which builds the organizational skill set and trust. Next, the **Innovation Committee** and **Strategic Alignment** steps ensure that AI initiatives are prioritized, resourced, and closely tied to key business goals. The fifth step, **POC Funding**, turns validated ideas into pilot projects. Together, these five layers create the robust technical, cultural, and organizational infrastructure necessary to move beyond isolated experiments and successfully scale AI projects into **Production**, where they can deliver maximum business value and transformation across the entire enterprise.

CHAPTER 3

Data Readiness—The Foundation of AI Success

Today, a company's data is everywhere; it is an ocean. Some data sources are wide, while others are deep. The data sits in a myriad of formats and locations. It lives in various SaaS products, including ERP, HRIS, Collaboration Suite, Sales, and Marketing software. Then there are the local file shares, servers, data warehouses, databases, and IOT devices. Today, it is neither cost-effective nor feasible to move all data to a single place. Forward-thinking enterprises recognize that data, when properly governed and managed, transcends its traditional role as a mere byproduct of operations. These organizations treat data as a high-value product that is reusable. It is a strategic asset capable of supporting a multitude of outcomes over an extended period rather than being restricted to a single project, operation, or team. This approach, known as Data-as-a-Product (DaaP), is essential for harnessing the full potential of accumulated organizational data, which spans digital records, documentation, and data sets.

From Project-Centric Costs to Product-Centric Assets

The traditional approach views data initiatives as project-centric endeavors. These efforts have defined endpoints and are often judged solely on meeting short-term metrics, such as being delivered on time and under budget. This mindset frequently leads to the creation of fragmented, siloed data assets lacking consistent quality and governance, resulting in significant bottlenecks and difficulties in scaling analytics.

The DaaP model necessitates a fundamental cultural shift within the organization. It institutionalizes data assets with a defined lifecycle and sustained investment, treating them as strategic assets that continuously deliver value. This transformation demands moving beyond the bare minimum of delivering requirements and fostering a deeper sense of accountability and ownership among dedicated product teams, ensuring they genuinely care about the data consumer's experience.

The inherent stability of product teams, compared to temporary project teams that disband upon completion, generates significant downstream benefits. Stability in team composition allows personnel to consistently work with the same assets and colleagues, enabling them to borrow from shared, continuously growing expertise rather than starting over repeatedly. This continuous engagement facilitates a deeper understanding of the market, the customers (internal and external), and competitive pressures. Consequently, these stable, product-focused teams can assess changing conditions far more rapidly and make better data-based recommendations, translating organizational stability directly into heightened organizational agility and responsiveness.

Furthermore, for large and complex organizations, relying on a monolithic, centralized data team often creates severe bottlenecks, struggling to keep up with the diverse demands of the business and lacking intimate knowledge of every source domain. The DaaP approach resolves this scaling dilemma by decentralizing ownership to domain experts. When implemented using principles like data mesh, DaaP allows analytic adoption to scale autonomously, moving beyond the capacity constraints of a single, centralized platform team.

DaaP is a holistic methodology rooted in product management principles, emphasizing data quality, usability, and user satisfaction. The ultimate objective is to transform raw data into a structured, accessible, and valuable product that is designed, built, and maintained with the specific needs of its end-users (internal employees, external customers, or partners) in mind.

To successfully launch this strategy, data initiatives must clearly align with real business problems and overarching company objectives. The foundational structure requires the Data and Analytics Leader to champion the cultural change and define the various forms of Data and Analytics products necessary for the enterprise. This leadership is responsible for establishing clear standards and a comprehensive framework governing the entire lifecycle: ideating, developing, deploying, scaling, and, eventually, retiring data products.

Case Study Snapshot: Leveraging DaaP for Competitive Advantage

Numerous large organizations demonstrate the transformative power of DaaP across various business outcomes:

- **Improved Customer Satisfaction and Added Revenue (Netflix):** Netflix utilizes data as a product via its sophisticated personalized content algorithm. By rigorously monitoring consumption patterns and behavioral trends, the company deploys customer-focused AI to recommend content tailored to individual interests, enhancing the user experience similar to a "helpful video-store clerk."[1] This personalization is crucial for maximizing user engagement, increasing customer loyalty, and ultimately driving retention and subscription revenue.

- **Model Accuracy and Operational Efficiency (Bank of America):** In the financial services sector, high-quality data products are leveraged for automated decision-making processes, such as fraud detection. By implementing robust data analytics, institutions like Bank of America have achieved direct, measurable cost savings by cutting fraud losses by half, demonstrating the value of improved predictive model accuracy.[2]

Cataloging the Data Product

To effectively implement and reinforce the DaaP strategy, organizations must transition data ownership and discovery from tribal knowledge to a formal, accessible system. This systematic approach is built upon a meticulous catalog of all key data flows and assets.

The data product catalog is not merely an inventory; it serves as the essential, centralized, and searchable marketplace for all enterprise data assets. This catalog is paramount for self-service, especially in decentralized data mesh architectures, as it enables consumers across various organizational domains to identify, understand, and access data assets efficiently.

A high-functioning catalog must move beyond basic technical documentation. It requires the collection and presentation of **active metadata**—information that is automatically collected and continuously updated. Active metadata includes operational insights such as data quality metrics, lineage, classification details, performance metrics, and usage statistics (e.g., popularity and top users). This rich, active metadata acts as the nexus of trust, empowering data consumers to independently verify the suitability and trustworthiness of a data product before they use it, thereby transforming data consumption from a high-friction request process to a seamless, self-service model. Historically, data engineers struggled because data was incomplete or riddled with errors, and they lacked contextual knowledge of the source domains. The catalog solves this by providing the necessary trust layer, ensuring consumers have the context needed to drive action based on accurate and complete information.

A comprehensive data product catalog must detail critical attributes for each data stream. These attributes are foundational for managing data product health, compliance, risk, governance, and usability:

- **Source System Identification**

  Identifying the origin of the data (the source system) is crucial for understanding its complete lineage and potential biases. This identification dictates the initial point of data quality control. Documenting the generating system (e.g., ERP, specific IoT sensor stream, CRM API endpoint, EDR telemetry) informs data engineers about upstream adjustments needed when data anomalies or integrity issues are detected.

- **Refresh Rate Documentation**

  Documenting how frequently the data is updated provides insights into its currency and determines its suitability for various use cases, particularly real-time or near-real-time applications. For large, performance-critical data products, it is vital to distinguish between a *full refresh* (a complete flush and reload of the data), an *incremental refresh* (which processes only a subset of data based on time-based rules), or real-time (data on demand via an API call). Incremental refresh process or real-time API calls are crucial for optimizing resource consumption and achieving faster update times, especially for high-velocity data products.

- **Sensitivity Level Classification**

   Classifying data by its sensitivity level is paramount for ensuring compliance with global privacy regulations (such as GDPR, CCPA, and HIPAA) and implementing appropriate security measures. Data is typically categorized into high, medium, or low sensitivity, often mapped to organizational labels such as Restricted/ Confidential (High), Sensitive/Internal Use Only (Medium), and Unrestricted/Public (Low).

   Data classification must explicitly address protected information, including Personally Identifiable Information (PII), Protected Health Information (PHI), financial records (PCI), and intellectual property. A core best practice mandates that if a database or resource includes data classified at two different levels, the entire data set must be classified at the highest sensitivity level present. This ensures adherence to the principle of least-privileged access controls, limiting internal use based on employee roles, and enforcing strict data access management.

- **Downstream Users and Applications**

   Understanding who consumes the data and for what purposes reveals the data product's impact across the entire organization. This documentation maps consumption across critical analytical models. This could produce a pipeline to executive dashboards, customer portals, and operational systems. This mapping is vital for effectively prioritizing data quality and reliability initiatives, ensuring that maintenance and resource allocation decisions are based on the highest business impact.

- **Impact of Disruption Assessment**
  Assessing and documenting the potential business impact should the data flow be interrupted or cease entirely is a critical yet often overlooked aspect of governance. This assessment must quantify the financial implications (e.g., estimated hourly revenue loss, brand reputation, estimated hourly productivity loss), operational disruptions, and risks to compliance or decision-making. It requires defining the Recovery Time Objective (RTO), establishing the maximum acceptable time for a data service to be unavailable. This attribute forms the essential basis for establishing formal Service Level Agreements (SLAs) and Data Contracts with downstream users, ensuring that upstream dependencies are accounted for when setting reliability targets.

Data Product Catalog Attribute Mapping and Rationale

Attribute	Purpose (Why It Matters)	Actionable Documentation Detail	Associated Risk/ Compliance
Source System	Verifies lineage and initial quality/bias	System name (e.g., SAPERP01), API endpoint, data generator owner, ingestion method	Data integrity, vendor management, auditing
Refresh Rate	Determines data currency and suitability for high-velocity use cases	Frequency (e.g., 5-minute stream), refresh type (full/ incremental)	Suitability for real-time decisions, SLA adherence (timeliness)
Sensitivity Level	Dictates necessary security and access controls	Classification label (e.g., PHI, PII, Restricted/ Confidential)	Regulatory fines (GDPR/HIPAA), intellectual property loss

Attribute	Purpose (Why It Matters)	Actionable Documentation Detail	Associated Risk/ Compliance
Downstream Users	Prioritizes maintenance and resource allocation	List of consuming teams/applications, critical ML models, dashboards	Scope of business impact if quality degradation occurs
Impact of Disruption	Quantifies financial and operational risk	Defined Recovery Time Objective (RTO), estimated hourly financial loss, and compliance reporting window failure	Business continuity, customer churn, regulatory reporting failure

Establishing Ownership

Beyond mere Cataloging, establishing clear and explicit ownership is essential for DaaP success. This requires dedicated roles and standardized responsibility matrices.

The Data Product Owner (DPO) is the central figure accountable for maximizing the user value derived from the data product through the efforts of the individual contributors. The DPO serves as the crucial bridge between data technology implementation and the desired business outcomes.

The DPO's mandate encompasses the entire product lifecycle. This includes gathering user requirements, defining the "why" (the underlying business problem), and advocating for the needs, wants, and aspirations of the end-users. They are responsible for setting the product strategy, developing the roadmap, and overseeing product development.

Crucially, the DPO is instrumental in governance and compliance. While they often coordinate requirements with dedicated security and compliance teams, the DPO is ultimately accountable for ensuring that the data product adheres to all relevant regulations, including establishing necessary access controls and privacy policies.

The implementation of DaaP frequently encounters organizational culture change challenges, particularly resistance from established departments fearing a loss of control or competitive advantage when data is shared freely. Due to this, the DPO must function as a political mediator and change manager. They must proactively foster collaboration across functional lines, clearly demonstrating the overarching benefits of DaaP to overcome internal inertia. To ensure effective adoption, the DPO must treat internal data consumers like customers, focusing on user experience, providing seamless onboarding, and offering continuous support to maximize engagement with the data product.

High-quality data product development and maintenance are managed by cross-functional, autonomous "squads," with each team accountable for all aspects of its specific domain. These teams are composed of individuals with distinct roles:

- **Data Product Owner:** holds central accountability for the product
- **Project Manager/Scrum Master:** orchestrates the team's workflow
- **Data Engineers:** handle data ingestion and modeling
- **Data Scientist:** required for products incorporating AI or analytics
- **Data Domain Steward/Architect:** provides expertise on the specific nature of the data type

Adopting organizational structures, such as empowering small, self-managing units, ensures that these cross-functional teams own the entire development process for their specific feature or data domain. This autonomy accelerates the time-to-market for data assets and fosters the deep sense of ownership necessary for maintaining product quality.

To guarantee explicit accountability, particularly for sensitive governance tasks, defining a Responsibility Assignment Matrix (RACI) is paramount. The RACI model clarifies who is Responsible (R—those who perform the work), Accountable (A—the single person ultimately answerable for the correct completion), Consulted (C—subject matter experts whose opinions are sought), and Informed (I—those kept up-to-date on progress or decisions). Applying RACI to data governance clarifies responsibilities, improves accountability, and reduces conflicts and confusion in complex, cross-functional tasks.

Essential Technology Stack Components

A robust implementation of DaaP requires a modern, integrated technology stack that supports the principles of domain ownership, self-service, and strong governance.

- **Data Catalogs and Discovery Tools:** As discussed, the data catalog is vital for discovery, enabling users to efficiently locate the exact data they need via searchable libraries and detailed metadata displays.
- **Data Platforms and Infrastructure:** Core platform services, such as AWS Lake Formation, Google BigQuery, Informatica, and orchestration layers such as Boomi, ClockSpring, and BetterCloud, are essential for building the data mesh pattern at scale. These tools provide the necessary infrastructure for sharing, hosting, cataloging data products, and enforcing tag-based access control.
- **Governance and Access Management:** Technology must support the implementation of encryption, access controls, and data governance frameworks. This includes tools that continuously categorize, inventory, and map data to confirm it receives the appropriate level of protection and enforces the least-privileged access policy based on user roles.

Fostering a data culture ensures continuous effort, commitment, and improvement. Establishing rigorous data quality controls is crucial for identifying problem areas, verifying the strengths and weaknesses of data methods, and moving away from opaque and inconsistent data handling practices. The Data Product Owner must ensure processes are in place to monitor data product health continuously and drive proactive improvements.

Executive Recommendations

The transformation of corporate data into high-leverage products is a strategic necessity that elevates data from a cost center byproduct to a scalable engine for business innovation. This holistic framework requires executive sponsorship and methodical implementation across three interconnected pillars:

1. **Establishing Trust through the Data Product Catalog:** Success depends on meticulously Cataloging data flows with rich, active metadata, detailing lineage, currency (refresh rate), sensitivity, and critical impact of disruption. This catalog must function as the definitive, single source of truth, enabling self-service and independent verification of data quality.

2. **Defining Accountability through Ownership and RACI:** Explicit ownership must be assigned via the DPO, who manages the entire product lifecycle and mediates organizational change. The RACI framework is non-negotiable for clarifying granular responsibilities, especially concerning data quality resolution and governance activities, ensuring that every critical deliverable has a single accountable party.

3. **Measuring Value through Business Outcomes:** The contribution of data products must be rigorously tracked and measured against quantifiable business outcomes, including added revenue (e.g., lead scoring efficacy), improved model accuracy (e.g., fraud loss reduction), enhanced operational efficiency (e.g., accelerated time-to-insight), and improved customer satisfaction (e.g., reduced churn).

By adopting this comprehensive, product-centric framework, organizations transform raw data assets into a powerful, measurable, and competitive advantage that sustains strategic enterprise success. The shift requires organizational commitment to decentralized accountability, rigorous governance, and continuous iteration guided by business value.

Transforming an organization through AI is a gradual process, not an overnight endeavor. A common misconception is that all an organization's data must be consolidated under a comprehensive DaaP framework for AI initiatives to succeed. While a well-structured data ecosystem is undeniably beneficial, it's more crucial to address and establish robust data governance and framework early in the AI project lifecycle.

Specifically, as AI initiatives progress into the POC phase, a foundational step involves defining clear data concerns and establishing appropriate data frameworks. This proactive approach ensures that data quality, accessibility, security, and ethical considerations are addressed from the outset. By setting these parameters early on, organizations can mitigate potential roadblocks and complexities that often arise when moving from experimental AI models to full-scale production. This strategic foresight ultimately paves the way for a much smoother and more successful transition into a production environment, maximizing the impact and return on investment of AI initiatives.

CHAPTER 4

The AI-Empowered Workforce:
Establishing Enterprise AI Literacy and Driving Departmental Adoption

The transformation promised by artificial intelligence systems is contingent not on the sophistication of the models themselves but on the ability of the human workforce to effectively engage with and steer them. Successful scaling is fundamentally reliant on the willingness and ability of employees to adopt new AI tools and workflows. Establishing deep organizational AI literacy acts as the essential accelerator, building a culture that is receptive to change and thereby dramatically increasing the speed of adoption. This chapter asserts that foundational AI training, coupled with highly customized and continuous learning pathways, is the single most critical investment an organization can make to bridge the gap between AI pilot projects and enterprise-wide transformative success.

The Cultural and Strategic Foundation for Adoption: The Imperative of AI Literacy

Integrating AI successfully within any enterprise necessitates a foundational cultural shift. This shift is not merely about introducing new tools; it is about redefining the strategic relationship between human talent and algorithmic systems. It is also explained that every new technology (e.g., cotton gin, telegraph, telephone, email, iPhone) has eliminated or changed jobs, but they also created jobs. Take the example of email. No longer do companies have secretaries who take shorthand and type everything for executives. Executives now send their own emails. Secretaries have been replaced by executive assistants.

Leaders must consistently articulate that AI is designed to augment rather than replace human capabilities. This strategic framing is critical because it directly addresses pervasive employee anxieties and cultural resistance that often stall technology adoption. AI must be positioned as an employee's co-pilot, which enhances productivity and enables employees to work on more strategic and creative tasks. Data suggests this cultural aspect is indeed the primary barrier to progress; nearly two-thirds (67%) of UK business leaders report that internal resistance and cultural barriers are actively stalling the rollout of pilot AI projects.[1]

Furthermore, AI literacy must be viewed through a psychological lens, extending beyond mere technical proficiency. High levels of AI literacy can contribute to a greater sense of psychological safety and efficacy among employees as the technology is demystified. Faculty members, for instance, who demonstrate higher AI literacy report greater competence and control in navigating digital environments, which enhances their engagement and fulfillment in their professional roles.[2] Several studies have linked employees with high AI literacy to utilizing applications more effectively, leading to increased productivity and efficiency. The inverse effect is equally profound. Disparities in technological readiness can lead to information overload, anxiety, and emotional exhaustion, factors that actively detract from overall job satisfaction and performance.

The necessity of comprehensive training is underscored by the current adoption gap. While a significant portion of enterprises report experiencing AI-driven productivity improvements (66% of UK firms), a substantial majority (62%) are yet to tap into the full potential of the technology.[1] This failure to fully capitalize on AI capabilities highlights a critical lack of investment in workforce transformation. Most companies have not offered company-wide or role-specific AI training. This is a systemic shortfall that must be resolved to unlock competitive advantage. The immediate goal of initial training, therefore, is twofold: to build technical skill sets and to simultaneously mitigate organizational risk by addressing and reducing cultural friction and anxiety levels, ensuring business continuity as new systems are introduced.

Establishing the Foundational, Model-Agnostic Curriculum

To ensure enduring value, the initial AI training curriculum must be foundational and model-agnostic, meaning the concepts taught remain relevant regardless of the specific vendor or large language model (LLM) the company ultimately chooses.

The curriculum should begin by demystifying the core technology, providing a foundational understanding of what AI is, how it works, and its various applications, moving beyond jargon with relatable examples such as spam filters or voice assistants. Providing a bit of AI history by going back to the 1950s and Alan Turing, briefly discussing how Amazon used it in the 1990s and early 2000s to suggest products to purchase, and moving into what most people think of, which is Generative AI, should be the next topic. This should also include basic concepts of machine learning, natural language processing, and automation tools.

The training should then shift to the core skills necessary for success in an AI-enhanced workplace, emphasizing soft skills as much as technical know-how. As AI automates routine tasks, human capabilities such as critical thinking, ethical reasoning, and adaptability become immensely more valuable and necessary. Employees must learn not just *how* to use AI, but *when* and *why*. And they need to be able to have the notion of verification.

A cornerstone of successful AI integration within any organization lies in the meticulous establishment of foundational training programs coupled with clearly defined organizational guardrails and responsible use protocols. These proactive measures are not merely bureaucratic hurdles but essential safeguards designed to maximize the benefits of AI while mitigating inherent risks.

It is imperative that clear and comprehensive usage guidelines are set forth early in the AI adoption process. These guidelines must meticulously specify:

- **Permitted Data Usage:** Precisely which types of data can be utilized by AI systems, ensuring compliance with privacy regulations, intellectual property rights, and internal data governance policies. This includes explicit directives on handling sensitive, confidential, or proprietary information.
- **Workflow Integration:** How AI can effectively assist and enhance specific workflows within different departments. This involves identifying areas where AI can automate repetitive tasks, provide data-driven insights, or support decision-making, all while maintaining human oversight.
- **Approved Product Usage:** A definitive list of approved AI products, platforms, and tools that employees are authorized to use for processing company data. This prevents the proliferation of unvetted or insecure solutions that could compromise data integrity or security.

By establishing these guidelines upfront, organizations can effectively align their AI strategy with existing organizational risk frameworks. This proactive approach prevents governance from becoming an impediment to productive experimentation and innovation, instead fostering an environment of controlled and responsible exploration.

Beyond technical guidelines, educating employees about the inherent pitfalls and limitations of AI is absolutely essential. This education should specifically address:

- **Bias Perpetuation:** How AI systems can inadvertently perpetuate and even amplify biases inherited from the historical training data they are fed. This includes discussing the societal implications of such biases and the importance of diverse and representative datasets. Employees must be trained to recognize and challenge AI outputs that may reflect discriminatory patterns.
- **The Phenomenon of "Hallucination":** The well-documented tendency of AI, particularly large language models, to generate plausible-sounding but entirely fabricated information, often referred to as "hallucination." Employees need to understand that AI outputs are not inherently factual and must be critically evaluated.

This includes training on fact-checking and cross-referencing information.

- **Compromised Output Reliability:** The broader understanding that various factors, including data quality, model limitations, and malicious inputs, can compromise the reliability of AI-generated output. This fosters a healthy skepticism and prevents blind acceptance of AI results.

Fostering a critical mindset among employees is paramount to responsible AI use. This involves developing the ability to:

- **Assess AI-Generated Insights:** Objectively evaluate the veracity, relevance, and implications of information and recommendations provided by AI systems.
- **Flag Inconsistencies:** Identify and report any discrepancies, illogical conclusions, or potentially biased outputs from AI.
- **Avoid Blind Reliance on Algorithms:** Understand that AI is a tool to augment human capabilities, not replace critical thinking or human judgment. Decisions, especially those with significant impact, must always involve human oversight and accountability.
- **The 80% Rule:** Generative AI should aim to produce approximately 80% of the final product, serving as a foundational tool that eliminates the challenge of starting from a blank page. However, it is essential for each individual to personalize and refine the output.

By investing in comprehensive training and fostering a culture of critical evaluation, organizations can empower their workforce to leverage AI effectively and ethically, ensuring that the technology serves as a powerful enabler rather than an unforeseen risk.

Currently, numerous companies have adopted a platform for collaboration, most of which incorporate embedded AI functionalities. Therefore, it is imprudent to assume that corporate training will disregard this advancement. The subsequent section will delve into prompt engineering, a skill that can be imparted irrespective of the chosen platform. Robust prompt-writing practices will yield comparable outcomes across various

AI platforms, including but not limited to ChatGPT, Gemini, CoPilot, Claude, and future generations of AI technologies.

Mastering the Human-AI Interface:
The Art and Science of Prompt Engineering

To fully leverage the capabilities of generative AI and ensure its outputs are reliable, structured, and auditable for mission-critical business processes, employees must progress beyond basic conversational inputs and master advanced prompt engineering techniques. This proficiency is crucial for transforming AI from a rudimentary tool into a powerful, precise instrument.

Prompt engineering serves as the essential refining layer that guarantees high-quality and accurate model outputs. It extends far beyond merely posing a question in the user interface. Instead, it involves providing comprehensive contextual information, specific constraints, desired output formats, and examples to the AI model. This detailed guidance enables the AI to produce nuanced, precise, and relevant outputs that align perfectly with the user's intent and the requirements of complex business operations. Without advanced prompt engineering, the AI's responses can be generic, unhelpful, or even inaccurate, thereby undermining its potential value in critical applications.

Initial training must elevate prompt writing from a general competency of asking questions to a core business skill enabling business decisions. This involves teaching techniques that ensure consistency and relevance when leveraging LLMs to perform corporate tasks, such as summarizing meetings, drafting complex content, or automating specific reports. Effective training emphasizes several key principles of high-quality prompting.

- **Clarity and Specificity:** Using precise language and action verbs to define the task or question, avoiding ambiguous requests. Use verbs such as *recommend, create, design,* and *automate.*
- **Contextual Relevance:** Providing comprehensive background information, including relevant facts, data, or desired constraints (e.g., "Summarize the article in no more than three sentences").

- **Quantification:** Quantifying requests whenever possible to set boundaries and guide the response scope. Examples of boundaries or guides include "use a professional tone," "do not use buzz words," and "do not use passive voice."

Because prompt engineering is a dynamic skill, employees must be trained to engage in an iterative process, experimenting with different phrasings and structures and using the model's feedback loop to continuously refine their prompt design based on output quality.

Advanced Reasoning Techniques for Enterprise Reliability - Chain of Thought

Beyond fundamental prompting, advanced techniques are necessary for complex tasks common in regulated or analytical corporate environments. These methods guide the model toward structured reasoning, enhancing both accuracy and accountability. For instance, in a highly regulated industry like finance or healthcare, simple prompts might not suffice when dealing with sensitive data or critical decision-making. Advanced techniques like Chain-of-Thought prompting, where the model is encouraged to explain its reasoning step-by-step, can provide greater transparency and auditability, which are paramount in such fields. Similarly, Tree-of-Thought prompting can be employed for exploring multiple reasoning paths before arriving at a conclusion, a valuable approach for complex problem-solving where a single, direct answer might be insufficient or even misleading. These techniques not only improve the quality of the output but also allow human experts to scrutinize the model's internal logic, fostering trust and enabling more effective oversight. Furthermore, these advanced methods contribute to better model governance by making the AI's decision-making process more interpretable and controllable, thereby mitigating risks associated with black-box AI systems in critical applications.

Chain-of-Thought (CoT) is a prompt engineering technique that significantly enhances the reasoning capabilities of LLMs, especially for tasks involving multi-step logic. CoT simulates human-like reasoning processes by explicitly breaking down elaborate problems into manageable, sequential steps that lead to a conclusive answer.

In contemporary business applications, CoT reasoning transcends its initial role as a technique for generating more accurate responses from LLMs. It has evolved into a fundamental governance mechanism, crucial for ensuring transparency, accountability, and debuggability within AI-driven systems. By compelling the LLM to explicitly articulate its intermediate reasoning steps, CoT illuminates the model's internal logic, transforming an opaque process into an observable and traceable one. This transparency is not merely a beneficial feature; it is an indispensable requirement in high-stakes operational domains, such as highly regulated industries like finance and healthcare.

Consider, for example, the legal review process, where a single misinterpretation could have profound legal and financial ramifications. Or, in complex financial analysis, where tracing the precise path to a particular investment decision or risk assessment is essential for regulatory compliance, auditing, and demonstrating due diligence. In such environments, CoT provides an audit trail, allowing human experts to scrutinize each step of the AI's decision-making process. This capability is paramount for validating the model's output, identifying potential biases or errors, and, ultimately, establishing accountability for automated decisions.

CoT's superiority becomes particularly evident when tackling intricate problems that inherently benefit from transparent, logical clarity. For instance, in supply chain management, CoT can be employed to trace the ripple effects of an interruption, from the initial point of failure through every subsequent impact on production, logistics, and delivery. This granular visibility allows businesses to quickly pinpoint bottlenecks, understand the full scope of an issue, and devise more effective mitigation strategies. Similarly, in executing detailed financial projections, CoT enables the model to break down complex calculations into understandable components, demonstrating how various assumptions and data points contribute to the final forecast. This not only enhances the credibility of the projection but also allows financial analysts to stress-test specific variables and understand their individual impact.

Historically, CoT was perceived as an emergent capability, predominantly associated with the largest and most sophisticated LLMs due to their extensive training data and architectural complexity. However, significant advancements in instruction tuning have democratized this powerful technique. Smaller, more specialized enterprise models can now be effectively trained and fine-tuned to perform CoT reasoning, making this critical capability accessible across a broader range of AI deployments. This evolution solidifies CoT's position as a platform-independent requirement for training and deploying responsible and robust AI systems across various industries and applications, moving beyond a niche feature to a foundational principle in AI governance and operational integrity.

Role Prompting and Persona Setting

Role Prompting is an essential technique for ensuring that AI outputs align with professional standards and domain expertise. This technique assigns a specific persona to the LLM, such as "experienced legal analyst" or "chief marketing officer." Defining the persona guides the style, tone, and focus of its responses. By utilizing Role Prompting, enterprises can dramatically enhance the clarity, accuracy, and domain relevance of the text, ensuring outputs conform to organizational requirements, such as writing a complex technical specification or drafting a customer pitch email that adheres to established brand voice and style.

Prompt Chaining

Prompt Chaining is a technique where you break down a complex task into a sequence of smaller, manageable sub-tasks. The key feature is that the output of one prompt is automatically used as the input for the next prompt in the sequence, creating a structured flow of information and reasoning. It mimics the way a human breaks down a large problem into sequential steps.

Instead of sending one massive, complicated prompt, you create a series of distinct steps:

1. **Initial Prompt (Step 1):** You give the LLM the first small task.
   Example: "Summarize the key financial trends from the following five-page report."

2. **Output 1:** The LLM generates the summary.
3. **Intermediate Prompt (Step 2):** You send the LLM a second prompt that uses the output from Step 1.
   Example: "Based on the summary you just created, identify the single greatest risk and the single greatest opportunity."
4. **Output 2:** The LLM generates the risk and opportunity.
5. **Final Prompt (Step 3):** You send a final prompt using the output from Step 2.
   Example: "Draft a one-paragraph email to the CEO presenting the risk and opportunity you identified, using a formal and urgent tone."

Prompt chaining offers several significant advantages over trying to stuff all instructions into a single prompt:

Benefit	Explanation
Improves Accuracy	By focusing on one small task at a time, the model is less likely to get confused or "hallucinate" details. It concentrates its processing power on a narrow scope.
Handles Complex Tasks	It allows you to tackle problems that are too large or intricate for a single prompt, like multi-stage data analysis or content generation.
Overcomes Context Limits	It helps manage the LLM's **context window** (the maximum amount of text it can process at once) by processing information sequentially rather than all at once.
Enhances Control	You can inspect the intermediate output of each step and adjust the next prompt in the chain if needed, giving you granular control over the final result.
Enables Automation	It's the foundation for creating complex AI agents and automated workflows (often using tools like LangChain or custom scripts) that reliably execute multi-step business processes.

Few-Shot Prompting

Few-Shot Prompting is a technique where the LLM is provided with a small number of complete input-output examples (the "shots") directly within the prompt itself, before presenting the final question.

This is a form of In-Context Learning (ICL), where the model temporarily learns the specific task, style, and format from the examples without requiring any permanent fine-tuning or re-training.

A typical Few-Shot prompt follows this structure:

1. **Instruction:** (The general rule for the task.)
   Example: "Classify the following review text as either POSITIVE or NEGATIVE."

2. **Example 1 (Shot):** (Input and desired Output)
   Example: Review: "The product worked flawlessly, 5/5 stars."
   >POSITIVE

3. **Example 2 (Shot):** (Input and desired Output)
   Example: Review: "It broke on the first use; completely unusable."
   >NEGATIVE

4. **Final Query:** (The new input the model must classify.)
   Example: Review: "The packaging was nice, but the item itself was just average." >

Few-Shot Prompting should be used whenever a simple instruction (Zero-Shot) isn't enough to get the precise result you need. It is particularly effective for tasks that require pattern adherence, consistency, or domain-specific understanding.

Training programs should clearly distinguish between advanced methods like Chain-of-Thought (CoT) and Prompt Chaining. CoT focuses on in-depth analysis and solving complex problems by explicitly detailing logical steps within a *single* prompt. In contrast, Prompt Chaining involves iterative refinement through a sequence of multiple prompts to gradually construct a comprehensive answer. While not always necessary, using a persona can provide valuable context, especially when developing strategies and roadmaps. Few-shot learning is employed when specific reasoning is required.

Advanced Prompting Techniques

Technique	Primary Function in Enterprise	Example Business Task	Impact on Output Quality
Chain-of-Thought (CoT)	Facilitates multi-step, transparent reasoning for complex problem-solving	Calculating detailed cash flow projections or tracing the source of a supply chain disruption	Increased Change to: accuracy and clarity in logic, critical for auditing complex decisions
Role Prompting	Assigns a domain-specific persona to align style, tone, and domain focus	Drafting a policy summary for executive review (as a compliance officer) or writing a pitch email (as a top salesperson)	Higher relevance, appropriate professional tone, and reduced need for human refinement
Few-Shot Prompting	Provides specific input-output pairs to guide the desired pattern or format	Generating standardized weekly status reports or highly stylized legal documents	Ensures consistency and predictability, reduces divergence from established corporate formats, and improves nuanced edge cases

The Shift to Embedded Intelligence: Training for the Enterprise Ecosystem

The greatest opportunity for productivity gains lies in leveraging AI that is integrated into the operational flow of work, moving the focus from interacting with general-purpose, standalone LLMs (such as Gemini or ChatGPT) to utilizing AI embedded within core enterprise applications.

Training for Model Agnostic Application

Modern enterprises often utilize a multi-model strategy, orchestrating various large language models (e.g., GPT-5, Gemini) behind a unified corporate interface to select the best AI "brain" for a given task. This necessitates a model-agnostic approach to training, where the focus remains on the *capability*—for example, "how to generate an executive summary"—rather than the specific vendor or LLM executing the task. This strategy ensures that employee skills are durable and future-proofed against the rapid pace of AI model evolution.

A cornerstone of effective and trustworthy enterprise AI systems lies in their ability to "ground" their responses in organizational data. This crucial process ensures that AI systems do not operate in a vacuum of generic information but instead leverage the rich, secure, and proprietary knowledge base of the enterprise. Examples of such internal data include vast repositories like the Microsoft Graph, which integrates data from various Microsoft services, or specialized, proprietary SAP data that is critical to business operations.

For AI systems to be truly valuable and readily adopted within an organization, the grounding process must be thoroughly explained and understood by users. This transparency is paramount for building the necessary trust between users and the AI. By clearly demonstrating that the AI is relying on secure, internal, and proprietary knowledge—rather than potentially unreliable, public web data—organizations can instill confidence in the system's outputs.

This understanding of the AI's data sources offers several critical benefits:

- **Enhanced Data Security:** When AI systems are explicitly grounded in internal data, it significantly reduces the risk of data breaches or the exposure of sensitive information. Users can be assured that their proprietary information remains within the secure confines of the organization.

- **Reduced Likelihood of Hallucinations:** AI "hallucinations" refer to instances where the AI generates plausible-sounding but factually incorrect information. By anchoring the AI's responses in verified organizational data, the potential for these fabrications is drastically minimized, leading to more accurate and reliable outputs.

- **Reliable Assistant Based on Corporate Context:** Ultimately, the goal of enterprise AI is to act as a reliable assistant. Grounding ensures that the AI's recommendations, analyses, and responses are deeply embedded within the specific corporate context. This means the AI understands and operates according to the organization's unique processes, policies, and strategic objectives, making it a truly valuable and aligned resource.

In essence, the meticulous grounding of AI systems in enterprise-specific data is not merely a technical detail; it is a fundamental strategic imperative for fostering trust, ensuring data integrity, mitigating risks, and, ultimately, realizing the full potential of AI as a dependable and contextually aware asset within the modern enterprise.

A significant advancement in AI platforms is the emergence of Personalized Retrieval-Augmented Generation (RAG) applications, specifically designed as AI Research and Learning Assistants. These applications offer a dedicated, long-context workspace, revolutionizing how users interact with and extract knowledge from large volumes of information.

Each of the major AI platforms has developed its own iteration of this concept:

- **ChatGPT: Projects**
- **Microsoft Copilot: Pages (or Microsoft 365 Copilot Notebooks)**
- **Google: NotebookLM**
- **Anthropic (Claude): Projects**

The core functionality across these platforms is consistent: they provide users with the ability to upload a substantially larger number of documents than standard chat interfaces allow. This extended capacity transforms them into powerful knowledge bases, where users can conduct in-depth research by asking questions that are *exclusively* related to the uploaded documents. This eliminates the distraction and potential inaccuracy of broader domain information, ensuring that the AI's responses are precisely tailored to the user's specific context and uploaded content.

These RAG applications empower users to:

- **Deep Dive into Specific Datasets:** Researchers, analysts, and students can upload an entire library of papers, reports, or internal documents to explore a specific subject area without sifting through unrelated external information.
- **Generate Context-Specific Insights:** The AI can synthesize information from across multiple uploaded documents to provide coherent and contextually relevant answers, summaries, and analyses.
- **Accelerate Learning and Understanding:** By having an AI assistant that can quickly process and interpret vast amounts of information directly relevant to their learning objectives, users can significantly accelerate their understanding of complex topics.
- **Improve Decision-Making:** For business users, these tools facilitate rapid access to institutional knowledge, project documentation, or market research, leading to more informed and data-driven decisions.

In essence, these personalized RAG applications represent a critical evolution in AI, shifting from general knowledge retrieval to highly specialized and context-aware information processing, making them indispensable tools for focused research, learning, and strategic analysis.

Training for Collaboration Suites (M365 Copilot and Google Gemini)

AI embedded within collaboration suites, such as Microsoft 365 Copilot and Google Gemini (in Workspace), represents a massive shift in daily productivity, providing assistance across documents, spreadsheets, email, and meeting platforms. Training for these suites must be highly platform-specific, emphasizing prompt generation that leverages cross-application context, such as asking the AI to summarize a team meeting based on a project plan contained in an attached document.

Effective deployment of these advanced AI collaboration tools necessitates a meticulously segmented adoption strategy, designed to cater to the distinct needs and responsibilities of various employee groups across the organization. This tailored approach ensures maximum impact, seamless integration, and robust security.

- **Champions and Adoption Managers:** These pivotal individuals are the vanguards of AI integration within their respective teams. Their training must extensively cover the "human change" aspect of technology adoption. This includes strategies for driving healthy, ethical, and productive usage of AI tools, fostering a culture of innovation, and overcoming resistance to change. A critical component of their role is identifying high-impact use cases that directly address team-specific challenges and opportunities, thereby demonstrating tangible value. Furthermore, they require comprehensive training in utilizing established frameworks and metrics to rigorously measure user satisfaction, track the time-to-value of AI implementations, and quantify improvements in efficiency and productivity. This allows for continuous optimization and showcases the return on investment for AI initiatives.

- **IT Professionals and Administrators:** This group forms the bedrock of secure and compliant AI deployment. Their specialized training must be hyper-focused on ensuring infrastructure readiness, which encompasses assessing existing systems, upgrading hardware and software where necessary, and establishing scalable architectures to support AI workloads. A paramount concern is robust security posture management, including the implementation of advanced threat detection, access controls, and data encryption protocols. Given that these AI collaboration suites often process and leverage highly sensitive organizational data, training must rigorously enforce data exposure prevention strategies and comprehensive risk analysis within the AI Security Posture Management (AI-SPM) framework. This includes understanding and mitigating potential vulnerabilities, ensuring compliance with relevant data privacy regulations (e.g., GDPR, CCPA), and establishing protocols for incident response.

- **Developers:** For developers, training needs to transcend basic usage, focusing instead on how to optimize and significantly extend the functionality of core AI tools like Copilot or Gemini.

This involves delving into advanced API integrations, custom model development, and the creation of bespoke applications that leverage the AI's capabilities. A key area of focus is enabling broader, cross-organizational scenarios, often through the strategic use of tools like Microsoft Graph connectors or similar integration platforms. These connectors allow developers to link the AI to a myriad of custom data sources (e.g., proprietary databases, internal knowledge repositories) or third-party business applications (e.g., CRM systems, ERP platforms), unlocking new efficiencies and enabling more intelligent, data-driven workflows across the enterprise. Training should also cover best practices for prompt engineering, model fine-tuning, and ensuring the ethical and responsible development of AI-powered solutions.

By embedding powerful, governed AI directly into the tools employees use daily, organizations provide an immediate, secure alternative to external, unapproved models (often referred to as Shadow IT), thereby containing significant security and compliance risks.

Integrating AI into Mission-Critical Systems (ERP, HRIS, CRM)

The integration of AI into Enterprise Resource Planning (ERP), Human Resource Information Systems (HRIS), and Customer Relationship Management (CRM) marks the final stage of comprehensive enterprise AI adoption. In these systems, AI provides "contextual intelligence" by integrating insights directly into the applications where work happens, eliminating the need for employees to navigate between systems.[2]

The contemporary business landscape is undergoing a profound transformation, necessitating a fundamental shift in how organizations approach employee development. This evolution demands comprehensive training programs specifically focused on **Augmented Intelligence**. Rather than replacing human intellect, Augmented Intelligence leverages advanced AI capabilities, such as SAP's Joule, to act as sophisticated, role-based assistants. These intelligent agents are designed to orchestrate and coordinate tasks across various critical business functions, including supply chain management, finance, and human resources. By seamlessly connecting disparate processes and providing real-time insights, these AI-powered assistants significantly accelerate workflows and directly contribute to the achievement of key business outcomes.

Furthermore, this technological paradigm shift requires that training initiatives also empower employees to effectively manage **hyperautomation**. Hyperautomation represents a more advanced stage of AI integration, where artificial intelligence is deeply embedded within an organization's operational fabric to automate a vast array of business processes. While the goal is to optimize efficiency and reduce manual effort, the successful implementation of hyperautomation fundamentally relies on human oversight, verification, and strategic intervention skills. Employees must be equipped to monitor automated processes, identify potential anomalies, troubleshoot issues, and make informed decisions when exceptions or complex scenarios arise. This necessitates a workforce capable of understanding the intricacies of AI-driven systems, discerning when human judgment is indispensable, and strategically guiding the evolution and application of automated solutions. Therefore, training must not only focus on the technical aspects of these tools but also cultivate critical thinking, problem-solving, and ethical decision-making abilities within an increasingly automated environment.

As AI rapidly integrates into the fundamental operations of businesses, its decisions are becoming inextricably linked to core business functions. This is evident in critical areas such as inventory reordering within ERP systems, where AI optimizes stock levels and supply chains, and resource allocation in HRIS, where AI streamlines workforce management and talent deployment. This increasing reliance on AI necessitates a proportional increase in the demand for, and comprehensive training on, Explainable AI (XAI) within these systems.

It is no longer sufficient for employees to simply accept the decisions that AI reaches; they must be trained on *how* and *why* those decisions were made. This emphasis on transparency and interpretability is crucial for several reasons:

- **Ensuring Transparency:** Understanding the decision-making process of AI fosters trust and clarity, allowing employees to confidently utilize AI-driven insights and outputs.
- **Promoting a Culture of Accountability:** When the rationale behind AI decisions is clear, individuals can better understand their role in the overall process and take responsibility for outcomes, whether they are directly interacting with the AI or managing its impact. This also enables better oversight and auditing of AI systems.
- **Maintaining Data Integrity:** By understanding how AI processes and uses data to arrive at its conclusions, organizations can identify potential biases, errors, or anomalies in the data inputs or the AI's logic, thereby safeguarding the accuracy and reliability of their information.

The critical importance of XAI is particularly pronounced in sectors where AI decisions have significant, real-world consequences. For instance:

- **Finance:** In the financial sector, AI plays a pivotal role in loan acceptance and rejection. XAI is essential to ensure that decisions are fair, unbiased, and compliant with regulatory requirements, providing clear explanations to applicants and stakeholders.
- **Education:** In admissions processes, AI can analyze vast amounts of applicant data. XAI is crucial to ensure that admissions decisions are equitable, justifiable, and free from discrimination, providing transparency to applicants and educational institutions.
- **Healthcare:** AI is increasingly used in healthcare, for example, in claim rejections. XAI is vital here to provide clear and understandable reasons for claim denials, ensuring fairness for patients and providers and facilitating accurate and ethical healthcare delivery.

The proliferation of AI across industries demands a proactive and comprehensive approach to XAI training, ensuring that human oversight and understanding remain at the forefront of AI integration.

Architecting Departmental AI Training: Tailoring the Curriculum

Generic, one-size-fits-all training is fundamentally insufficient for achieving meaningful AI adoption. Training must be highly practical, targeted, and specifically designed around the diverse roles, responsibilities, functional workflows, and unique risk profiles present across the organization.

The requirement for customized training is not merely a best practice; it is increasingly a regulatory necessity. Article 4 of the European Union's AI Act mandates that providers and deployers of AI systems ensure that their employees and third parties possess a "sufficient level of AI literacy." This AI literacy is explicitly defined as the "skills, knowledge, and understanding" necessary for employees to make an informed and responsible deployment of AI systems, along with an awareness of potential risks and opportunities.[4] Organizations must proactively define *how* specific groups will use *which* AI systems and provide the necessary training to ensure that use is compliant and risk-aware.

Beyond adhering to EU mandates regarding AI ethics and data privacy, a crucial next step involves comprehensive training for various departments on the specific applications and tools available to them. This training should not merely focus on theoretical concepts but rather on practical, hands-on demonstrations and activities of how AI can enhance their daily operations.

Empowering employees with insights into "the art of the possible" is paramount. This means showcasing a wide array of successful AI implementations across different industries and functions, sparking their imagination and encouraging them to think creatively. Through such exposure, employees can begin to identify specific challenges within their own workflows that AI could address, leading to the development of tailored use cases. This approach fosters an environment of innovation where employees are not just consumers of AI tools but active participants in extending their utility far beyond the initial training parameters. This continuous exploration and application will be key to maximizing the return on investment in AI technologies and embedding an AI-first mindset throughout the organization.

Furthermore, it involves an in-depth examination of the existing platforms acquired for employees. Many of these platforms offer extensive capabilities such as research, image and video generation, email summarization, and note-taking, with this list continually expanding. Training should not only cater to departmental needs but also demonstrate how to effectively utilize current tools specifically for each department. The objective is to maximize both employee productivity and the return on investment in company platforms. This dual investment in both human capital and technological infrastructure warrants recognition.

Designing the curriculum requires segmenting training based on the functional responsibilities and mission-critical applications of each department. This ensures employees can immediately grasp the practical relevance and value of AI in their daily tasks, thereby accelerating the integration phase and mitigating adoption resistance.

Finance

Finance departments leverage AI for predictive analytics, complex financial modeling, fraud detection, and high-volume document processing. Their training must focus heavily on the integrity of inputs and the auditability of outputs. Key focus areas include interpreting sophisticated model outputs, understanding the limitations and potential biases of forecasting algorithms, and rigorously assessing data quality. Because financial processes are highly regulated, specialized training on Explainable AI principles is paramount, ensuring that the logic behind any AI-driven decision, such as a credit approval or fraud flag, is clear, auditable, and compliant. Furthermore, CoT prompting techniques are required for complex, multistep analysis tasks that demand explicit logical clarity.

In today's rapidly evolving technological landscape, Enterprise Resource Planning (ERP) systems are increasingly integrating artificial intelligence functionalities. For the Financial Planning & Analysis (FP&A) team, a comprehensive understanding of these AI capabilities and their limitations is paramount. This knowledge is not merely academic; it is

crucial for strategically leveraging AI to optimize and automate traditionally labor-intensive processes within the finance function.

Specifically, the FP&A team should focus on how AI within their ERP
system can be harnessed for:

- **Invoice Matching:** AI-powered systems can significantly streamline the invoice matching process, which often involves reconciling
  purchase orders, goods receipts, and vendor invoices. By automating this, the system can identify discrepancies, flag potential
  errors, and even process straightforward matches without human
  intervention, freeing up valuable human resources for more complex analysis.

- **Anomaly Detection:** The ability of AI to detect anomalies in
  financial data is a powerful tool for risk management and fraud
  prevention. AI algorithms can identify unusual patterns, outli-
  ers, or deviations from expected norms in large datasets, such
  as unexpected spikes in expenses, unusual transaction volumes,
  or discrepancies in revenue recognition. Early detection of such
  anomalies can prevent financial losses and ensure data integrity.

- **Predictive Forecasting:** AI significantly enhances the accuracy
  and efficiency of financial forecasting. By analyzing historical data,
  market trends, economic indicators, and other relevant variables,
  AI models can generate more precise revenue forecasts, expense
  predictions, and cash flow projections. This allows the FP&A team
  to move beyond traditional, often manual, forecasting methods
  to a more dynamic and data-driven approach, enabling better
  strategic planning and resource allocation.

By understanding the "what it does and does not do" of their ERP's
AI features, FP&A professionals can proactively identify opportunities for
automation, improve data accuracy, mitigate risks, and ultimately provide
more insightful and timely financial guidance to their organizations. This
strategic engagement with AI is no longer a luxury but a necessity for modern FP&A teams aiming for operational excellence and strategic influence.

Finance and accounting teams are increasingly empowered by the
integration of sophisticated tools within modern collaboration platforms.

These comprehensive suites of applications provide the capabilities necessary to move beyond basic data entry and reporting, enabling in-depth financial analysis and strategic planning.

Key functionalities include:

- **Meticulous Analysis of Complex Spreadsheets:** Teams can leverage powerful spreadsheet applications with advanced functions, pivot tables, and data visualization tools to dissect intricate financial models and large datasets. This allows for the identification of trends, anomalies, and key performance indicators with greater precision.

- **Generation of Detailed Variance Reports:** Automated reporting features streamline the creation of comprehensive variance reports. These reports compare actual financial performance against budgets, forecasts, or prior periods, highlighting significant deviations and providing critical insights into operational efficiency and financial health. This enables proactive identification of areas requiring attention and informed corrective actions.

- **Development of Sophisticated "What-If Scenarios":** By utilizing scenario planning tools, finance professionals can build dynamic models to assess the potential financial outcomes of various strategic decisions. This includes modeling the impact of changes in market conditions, investment strategies, pricing structures, or operational efficiencies. Such capabilities are crucial for informed risk management and strategic decision-making, allowing organizations to anticipate challenges and capitalize on opportunities.

Sales and Marketing

Personnel in sales and marketing leverage AI tools, primarily integrated within Customer Relationship Management (CRM) systems, to significantly enhance their operational efficiency and strategic outreach. These AI capabilities automate and streamline a variety of tasks, including the generation of personalized customer recommendations, the execution of highly targeted outreach campaigns, and the creation of compelling content. Some of this could also be done within certain collaboration suites.

The training curriculum for these teams must therefore be meticulously designed to concentrate on boosting overall marketing performance and elevating the customer experience. Specific training areas are critical for maximizing the effectiveness of AI adoption. These include, but are not limited to:

- **Effective Prompt Writing for High-Impact Sales Messaging:** This segment will focus on developing the skills to craft precise and impactful prompts for generative AI. The goal is to produce sales messages that not only are persuasive but also resonate deeply with the target audience, leading to increased engagement and conversion rates.

- **Adhering to Brand Voice through Role Prompting:** Training will emphasize the importance of maintaining a consistent brand voice across all AI-generated content. This involves utilizing Role Prompting techniques, where AI models are instructed to adopt a specific persona or brand identity, ensuring that all communications align with the company's established tone, style, and values.

- **Ethical Use of Large Volumes of Customer Data:** A crucial component of the training will address the ethical considerations associated with processing and utilizing extensive customer data. This includes understanding data privacy regulations, obtaining proper consent, using anonymization techniques, and ensuring that AI applications respect customer boundaries and build trust.

- **Legal Risks Associated with Generative Content:** The curriculum must also thoroughly address the legal implications and risks inherent in the creation and deployment of generative content. This includes ensuring strict compliance with intellectual property laws, safeguarding against copyright infringement, and understanding potential liabilities related to AI-generated outputs. Training will cover best practices for content vetting, attribution, and risk mitigation strategies to avoid legal challenges.

Beyond the immediate functionalities of a CRM system, the collaborative environment within an organization presents a rich landscape for leveraging advanced tools. This begins with fundamental yet powerful capabilities such as meeting recordings, which ensures comprehensive documentation of discussions and decisions, and intelligent note-taking, which can automatically identify key action items and assignees.

Furthermore, these collaborative teams stand to significantly benefit from the strategic implementation of video generation tools. These tools offer the ability to craft compelling, smaller-scale campaigns with remarkable efficiency. This not only empowers teams to react swiftly to market trends but also crucially prevents an increased workload on already stretched design and creative departments. The scope of these tools can also extend to customizing larger, more intricate creative works, allowing for bespoke tailoring of content to resonate specifically with individual clients or market segments, thereby enhancing personalization and engagement.

Additionally, the integration of robust research capabilities embedded within major digital platforms provides an invaluable resource for market intelligence. These capabilities enable teams to delve deep into understanding new markets, identifying emerging customer segments, and gaining crucial insights into their needs and preferences. Concurrently, they facilitate the continuous maintenance of up-to-date information on existing customers, ensuring that engagement strategies remain relevant and effective. This continuous feedback loop of research and insight directly supports the creation of campaigns that not only are timely but also resonate with current market dynamics and consumer sentiments. By consistently feeding insights back into campaign development, organizations can ensure their messaging is always pertinent and impactful.

Human Resources

HR departments are increasingly leveraging AI-driven solutions integrated within Human Resources Information Systems (HRIS) to streamline various operations. These applications range from automating routine workflows to generating comprehensive job descriptions and employing sophisticated predictive analytics for employee retention modeling and talent acquisition. However, the deployment of these AI tools introduces significant challenges, primarily centered on ethical reasoning and the critical need for bias mitigation.

To address these challenges, comprehensive training programs are essential. Such training must focus on equipping HR professionals with the skills to identify and proactively address potential algorithmic biases embedded within hiring processes or performance evaluation models. Failure to do so could lead to unfair outcomes for employees, damage to organizational reputation, and significant legal liabilities. Furthermore, employees need to develop proficiency in applying explainable artificial intelligence techniques. This capability allows HR teams to understand the underlying drivers and rationale behind AI-generated predictions, such as those related to employee retention. This transparency fosters trust in the AI system and enables HR professionals to make more informed, data-driven decisions.

Beyond ethical considerations, robust training on data privacy and the responsible handling of sensitive employee information is absolutely non-negotiable. With AI systems processing vast amounts of personal data, organizations must ensure strict adherence to data protection regulations and best practices. This includes understanding consent protocols, data anonymization techniques, secure data storage, and strict access controls to prevent unauthorized access or misuse of employee data. The integrity and confidentiality of employee information are paramount, and any compromise in these areas can have severe consequences, undermining employee trust and leading to regulatory penalties. Therefore, continuous education and adherence to stringent data privacy policies are fundamental for the ethical and effective integration of AI into HR operations.

HR professionals can also use AI beyond their HRIS system. Through collaboration suites other labor-intensive workflows can be optimized. This includes onboarding/offboarding, employee support and requests, recruitment and hiring pipelines, and communications.

Onboarding requires coordination across HR, IT, and the hiring manager. Collaboration suites centralize and automate this coordination:

- **Automated Checklists & Task Assignment:** Use project management features (like in Asana or monday.com) to create a standard Onboarding Workflow Template. The collaboration tool automatically assigns tasks (e.g., IT to set up laptop, HR to send benefits packet, Manager to schedule 1:1s) and sets deadlines for each stakeholder.

- **Centralized Knowledge Hub:** Create a dedicated onboarding channel (Slack/Teams/Meets) or a shared internal wiki/document (Box/Notion/Google Drive). This becomes the single source of truth for the new hire's checklist, required forms, and links to training videos, eliminating the "where is that document?" problem.
- **Real-Time Q&A:** New hires can post questions in a public channel dedicated to "New Hire Q&A," allowing HR to answer once for everyone, reducing repetitive emails and encouraging peer-to-peer support.

Collaboration tools create a streamlined, trackable system for employee inquiries (Help Desk style):

- **Standardized Request Forms:** Use the integration features to connect a form builder (like Microsoft Forms, Google Forms, or specialized HR apps) to a dedicated HR Support Channel. Requests (e.g., time off, benefits question, payroll issue) are submitted through the form and automatically post as a structured task in the channel.
- **Tracking and Accountability:** The collaboration suite provides visibility on who owns the request, the current status, and the deadline, ensuring requests don't get lost in HR inboxes.
- **Self-Service Knowledge:** Human resources departments frequently receive repetitive, easily answerable, yet disruptive inquiries. Chatbots could address these straightforward questions. Implement a robust search function across shared documents (e.g., Google Drive, SharePoint, or a Notion HR Hub) so employees can quickly find answers to FAQs (e.g., "What is the holiday schedule?"), reducing direct inquiries to HR staff.

Hiring involves continuous collaboration among recruiters, hiring managers, and interviewers:

- **Interview Feedback Consolidation:** Create a temporary project or channel for a specific open role. Interviewers can quickly share feedback and ratings directly within the chat thread or linked document, keeping all comments centralized and tied to the specific candidate profile.

- **Scheduling:** Integrate calendar apps (Outlook, Google Calendar) directly into the chat tool. Recruiters can instantly see the availability of multiple interviewers and schedule complex panel interviews without leaving the collaboration platform.
- **Sourcing and Branding:** Use designated channels to share potential candidates, track successful referral programs, and coordinate employer branding campaigns with the Marketing team.

Collaboration suites help ensure information is consumed, understood, and tracked:

- **Targeted Announcements:** Use channels or tags to send policy updates only to the relevant groups (e.g., a specific update for "Sales Team" or "NY Employees"), minimizing information overload for the rest of the company.
- **Compliance Tracking:** Use reactions or automated acknowledgement prompts (available in tools like Teams) to get employees to confirm they have read and understood a new policy document, providing a lightweight compliance audit trail.
- **Real-Time Feedback:** Use built-in polls or discussion threads to solicit feedback on draft policies, making the process more collaborative and ensuring policies are practical for the wider workforce.
- **Employee Engagement:** Use video to explain how to walk through open enrollment, create welcome videos for new hires, create new hire onboarding videos to introduce standard tools and how to use them.

Legal and Compliance

Legal and compliance teams are at the forefront of navigating the intricate landscape of AI integration, necessitating specialized training focused on risk assessment and mitigation. Their curriculum must delve deep into the complexities of AI governance, equipping them with the expertise to meticulously review and summarize contractual risks associated with AI adoption. This includes a thorough understanding of regulatory compliance checks, ensuring that all AI applications adhere to local, national, and international laws and standards. A critical component of their training involves understanding the profound legal implications of model "hallucination," where AI generates incorrect or misleading information, and data leakage, which can expose sensitive information.

The training must instill a profound fluency in the organizational AI governance framework, clarifying established protocols for data security, privacy protection, and ethical AI deployment. It's imperative that these teams not only are aware of mandatory training requirements but also fully grasp and enforce AI compliance mandates across all departments. This comprehensive understanding ensures that AI initiatives are not only innovative but also legally sound and ethically responsible.

The inherent complexity of departmental risk exposure underscores the critical need for a clear understanding of inter-departmental dependencies. Consider a scenario where the human resources department deploys a biased AI model for hiring. Such a deployment immediately creates significant legal risk for the legal department, potentially leading to lawsuits and reputational damage.

Therefore, training modules must extend beyond departmental silos to include robust cross-functional awareness of data security and ethical dependencies. This approach prevents localized failures from escalating into enterprise-wide risk contagion. For instance, if an AI model used by marketing inadvertently collects and processes data in a non-compliant manner, it could create legal liabilities that impact the entire organization. By fostering a shared understanding of AI's ethical and security implications across departments from R&D to operations, sales, and customer service, the organization can establish a more resilient and responsible AI ecosystem. This integrated approach ensures that all stakeholders are equipped to identify, mitigate, and respond to AI-related risks collaboratively, safeguarding the organization's reputation, financial stability, and long-term strategic objectives.

Beyond the legal implications of simply implementing AI across the enterprise, legal teams can use AI to improve their workflows. Legal teams can transform their highly specialized and documentation-heavy workflows by integrating AI and LegalTech solutions directly into their collaborative suites (like Microsoft 365/Copilot or Google Workspace/ Gemini). The primary goal is to shift legal professionals from manual document review and triage to strategic analysis and judgment.

AI assistants embedded directly into document editors (Word, Google Docs) and collaboration platforms can accelerate the most time-consuming task: contract review.

Process	AI Use in the Collaboration Suite
Contract Drafting	Legal-specific AI (often integrated via Copilot/Gemini) generates the first draft of a standard document (e.g., NDA, Vendor Agreement) based on a simple prompt and pre-approved organizational templates.
Risk Flagging	AI automatically scans incoming third-party contracts (attached in email or shared in a channel) and flags clauses that deviate from the company's approved "playbook," drawing the attorney's attention only to high-risk areas like indemnity, termination, or privacy.
Clause Comparison	An attorney can highlight a clause and ask the AI: "Compare this clause to our standard termination clause and list all material differences," saving hours of manual comparison.
Summarization	Use the AI tool to instantly summarize the key terms and deadlines of a large PDF or legal document, allowing business partners to quickly grasp the essential information without waiting for a full legal review.

Collaboration suites manage the flow of work from the business to the legal department. AI can automate the first steps of triage:

- **Automated Intake:** A business partner submits a legal request form (e.g., a "New Contract Request") via a dedicated channel or form integrated with the suite (e.g., Jira Service Management, Microsoft Forms). AI immediately reads the form data to triage the request:
  » **Category:** *Contract Review, IP, Litigation.*
  » **Priority:** *High (deadline in 7 days), Medium, Low.*
  » **Routing:** Automatically assigns the matter to the correct specialist (e.g., Privacy Counsel or Commercial Counsel) and creates a trackable task.

- **Deadline Management:** AI agents (like those in Microsoft Copilot or Google Workspace Flows) monitor for key dates mentioned in emails or shared documents and automatically create calendar entries and reminders for attorneys and paralegals.

- **Email Summary:** For long email chains regarding a matter, the AI can instantly summarize the thread: "Catch me up on this vendor negotiation, highlighting the last 3 proposed changes." Several platforms are providing summaries for email conversations automatically.

E-Discovery and Case Management

While full e-discovery often uses specialized software, collaboration suites use AI to assist with the most time-consuming component: identifying relevant documents:

- **Search and Retrieval:** AI enhances search across the firm's shared files (SharePoint, Google Drive) by looking for **semantic meaning** rather than just keywords, helping legal teams quickly locate all related evidence, documents, and communications for a specific matter.

- **Transcription and Indexing:** For recorded meetings (Microsoft Teams, Google Meet), AI generates a **transcript and indexes key discussion points**, making video content searchable and reviewable for e-discovery purposes.

- **Privilege Screening:** Advanced legal AI tools can analyze large sets of internal communications (chats, emails) shared in the suite and flag potential **privileged communications** before they are accidentally shared.

Departmental AI Training Matrix: Use Cases and Skill Focus

Department	Key Embedded System (Example)	Primary AI Use Cases	Critical Training Focus & Risk Mitigation
Finance	ERP (SAP, Netsuite, PeopleSoft)	Predictive forecasting, budget variance analysis, automated reporting	Data lineage verification, Explainable AI (XAI) for decision transparency, regulatory oversight, CoT Prompting for complex analysis
HR	HRIS (Workday, SuccessFactors, ADP)	Retention modeling, talent acquisition, workflow automation	Bias mitigation in predictive models, ethical use of sensitive employee data, adherence to privacy regulations, interpretation of key retention drivers
Sales & Marketing	CRM (Salesforce, Zoho, Hubspot)	Personalized recommendations, automated customer outreach, content creation	Effective Role Prompting for tone, brand compliance, managing AI agents, and IP/copyright adherence for generated content
Legal & Compliance	Collaboration Suites, eDiscovery Tools	Contract summary and risk analysis, policy review, internal compliance checks	AI governance framework comprehension, data security protocols, legal implications of hallucination, compliance training

The Governance Layer: Compliance, Ethics, and Explainable AI (XAI)

For AI adoption to scale responsibly, initial training must integrate the organizational governance framework. Governance ensures that AI operates within ethical and legal boundaries, mitigating potential risks related to bias, privacy breaches, and security threats.

This will be an ever changing landscape. Various countries are at different stages of AI mandates. The EU AI Act confirms that AI literacy is a legal mandate, requiring employees to be aware of AI risks and possible harm.[1] Mandatory training must focus on mitigating the significant legal and ethical concerns raised by workplace AI, including potential discrimination, inherent bias, and violations of data privacy.[5]

Effective governance training necessitates the establishment of explicit policies, regulations, and data governance protocols. These measures are crucial for the proper monitoring, evaluation, and updating of algorithms, thereby mitigating flawed or harmful outcomes. By anchoring training within the established AI governance framework, organizations cultivate a culture where employees inherently grasp the imperative of utilizing AI ethically and responsibly, ensuring adherence to dynamic regulatory landscapes. Given the rapid pace of technological evolution, this compliance training cannot remain static; rather, it must function as a continuous feedback loop, consistently adapting to incorporate new AI capabilities, emergent risks, and regulatory amendments.

Quantifying the Return on AI Literacy Investment (ROALI)

To justify the significant commitment to comprehensive, customized training, organizations must adopt a robust measurement framework: the Return on AI Literacy Investment (ROALI). This framework must capture both short-term efficiency gains and long-term strategic value.

The strategic value of AI investment transcends the conventional metrics of Return on Investment (ROI), which typically emphasize cost savings. A more comprehensive and mature framework, termed Return on AI Led Innovation, is essential to accurately gauge the multifaceted benefits of AI. This framework must meticulously evaluate three critical dimensions:

- **Efficiency Gains:** This dimension encompasses the tangible improvements in operational processes and resource utilization. AI can automate repetitive tasks, optimize workflows, and enhance the speed and accuracy of various operations, leading to significant cost reductions and increased productivity. Examples include automated data entry, predictive maintenance in manufacturing, and AI-powered customer service chatbots that resolve queries more quickly.

- **Quality of Outputs:** Beyond mere efficiency, AI significantly elevates the quality and precision of an organization's deliverables. This can manifest in improved data analysis, more accurate forecasting, enhanced product design, and the development of more personalized customer experiences. For instance, AI in healthcare can assist in more accurate diagnoses, while in marketing, it can tailor content to individual preferences, leading to higher engagement and conversion rates.

- **Strategic Benefits:** This crucial dimension captures the broader, long-term advantages that AI confers, which are often overlooked in traditional ROI calculations. These benefits include:

  » **Enhanced Organizational Agility:** AI empowers organizations to respond more rapidly and effectively to market changes, competitive pressures, and emerging opportunities. By providing real-time insights and predictive analytics, AI enables proactive decision-making and fosters a more adaptive and resilient organizational structure.

  » **Innovation Acceleration:** AI serves as a powerful catalyst for innovation, enabling the development of novel products, services, and business models. From accelerating research and development cycles to identifying new market niches,

AI can unlock unprecedented opportunities for growth and differentiation.

» **Competitive Advantage:** Organizations that strategically leverage AI can gain a significant edge over competitors. This can stem from superior operational efficiency, enhanced product quality, or the ability to innovate at a faster pace, ultimately leading to market leadership and sustained growth.

» **Improved Decision-Making:** AI provides advanced analytical capabilities that enable more informed and data-driven decisions across all levels of an organization, reducing reliance on intuition and guesswork.

The ROALI calculation necessitates a transparent and exhaustive accounting of all investments. This extends beyond the immediately apparent expenditures such as licensing fees for AI software and infrastructure costs for hardware and cloud services. Critically, it must also incorporate the often-underestimated expense of workforce development. This includes:

- **Training Programs:** Committing to investing in comprehensive training programs to enhance employee competencies in AI-related fields, thereby ensuring their effective utilization and management of AI technologies, is neither a small nor quick task. This encompasses the development of department-specific training for internal platforms and dedicated time for team instruction. The cost associated with these initiatives will increase proportionally with the decentralization and geographical distribution of the enterprise.

- **Internal Mentorship:** Establishing mentorship initiatives where experienced AI practitioners guide and support less experienced colleagues, fostering knowledge transfer and skill development.

- **Developing Continuous Learning Materials:** Creating and maintaining a library of resources, tutorials, and documentation to support ongoing learning and adaptation to evolving AI landscapes.

- **Compliance Costs Associated with Data Readiness:** Ensuring data privacy, security, and ethical use in accordance with relevant regulations and industry standards. This involves investments in data governance frameworks, auditing processes, and legal counsel to navigate the complex landscape of AI ethics and compliance.

By adopting the ROALI framework, organizations can move beyond a simplistic view of AI as merely a cost-cutting tool and instead recognize its transformative potential as a strategic enabler of innovation, efficiency, and long-term competitive advantage.

Direct Value Metrics (Efficiency and Quality)

These metrics provide a direct assessment of the immediate impact resulting from the application of AI skills across various operational domains:

- **Efficiency Improvements:** This category emphasizes measurable improvements to operational processes. Key metrics include, but are not limited to, reductions in average handling times for tasks, substantial increases in throughput rates across various workflows, and demonstrable decreases in existing backlog volumes subsequent to the implementation and integration of AI-powered tools. For example, in customer service, AI-driven chatbots can significantly curtail response times, while in data processing, AI algorithms can expedite the analysis of extensive datasets, thereby minimizing manual effort and processing delays. Similarly, senior developers can leverage code-assisted AI to accelerate the introduction of new features into products.

- **Performance and Cost:** This area is dedicated to quantifying gains in overall productivity and the realization of labor efficiencies. Senior leadership frequently highlights how AI technologies free up valuable human capital, allowing employees to shift from routine, repetitive tasks to high-impact work. This includes activities such as driving innovation, fostering strategic planning, engaging in complex problem-solving, and developing new business opportunities. By automating mundane tasks, AI allows skilled personnel to focus on initiatives that contribute more directly to organizational growth and competitive advantage, ultimately leading to significant cost savings through optimized resource allocation and increased output per employee.

- **Risk Mitigation:** This metric measures the reduction in error rates for tasks that are either entirely performed by AI or significantly assisted by AI. Furthermore, it quantifies the financial savings derived from a decrease in fraud incidents, particularly in sectors like finance and cybersecurity, and a reduction in regulatory risks through enhanced compliance monitoring and automated adherence to industry standards. AI can meticulously analyze vast amounts of data to identify anomalies and potential compliance breaches much faster and more accurately than human analysis, thereby proactively preventing costly penalties, reputational damage, and legal complications.

Indirect Value Metrics (Strategic Outcomes)

The adoption and integration of AI literacy within an organization are not merely technical shifts; they represent a profound cultural transformation with long-lasting impacts. These impacts can be measured through various indicators that reflect changes in how employees work, innovate, and perceive their roles.

One of the most significant outcomes of increased AI literacy is a dramatic improvement in organizational agility and innovation. By automating repetitive or time-consuming tasks, AI frees up valuable employee time, allowing individuals and teams to redirect their focus toward more strategic, creative, and high-impact endeavors:

- **Speed and Volume of New Ideas:** A key metric here is assessing the rate at which new, impactful ideas are generated and implemented. This includes not only the quantity of ideas but also their quality, originality, and potential to drive business value. Organizations should track the number of successful new product launches, process improvements, or market expansions that can be directly attributed to the reallocated time and enhanced analytical capabilities enabled by AI.

- **Strategic Time Reallocation:** It is crucial to quantify the value generated from this redirected time. This involves analyzing how employees are utilizing their newly available bandwidth. Are they engaging in more complex problem-solving, developing innovative solutions, pursuing advanced research, or focusing on high-level strategic planning? The value can be measured by the financial returns, competitive advantages, or operational efficiencies gained from these strategic activities. This might involve tracking the ROI of projects initiated due to AI-freed time or assessing the impact of enhanced customer experiences and product development.

- **Cross-Functional Collaboration:** AI literacy often fosters a more collaborative environment. When teams are equipped with AI tools, they can more easily share data, insights, and predictive models, leading to more integrated and innovative solutions across departments. This can be measured by the frequency and success of cross-functional projects.

- **Proactive Problem Solving:** With AI handling routine tasks, teams can shift from reactive problem-solving to proactive identification of opportunities and potential challenges. This leads to more foresight in decision-making and a stronger capacity for anticipating market shifts.

Beyond organizational performance, AI literacy plays a critical role in enhancing individual employee efficacy, satisfaction, and, ultimately, retention. When employees are empowered with AI tools and the knowledge to use them effectively, their work experience is significantly improved:

- **Improved Employee Satisfaction and Engagement:** Monitoring improvements in employee satisfaction surveys can provide direct insights into the positive impact of AI literacy. Employees who feel competent in using AI tools to enhance their work often report higher job satisfaction, a greater sense of accomplishment, and increased engagement. The removal of tedious tasks allows them to focus on more rewarding aspects of their roles.

- **Enhanced Sense of Control and Autonomy:** AI literacy often gives employees a greater sense of control over their work. By leveraging AI to automate mundane aspects, they can prioritize their efforts on tasks that require human creativity, critical thinking, and interpersonal skills. This increased autonomy contributes to a more fulfilling work experience and a stronger sense of ownership over their contributions.

- **Reduced Burnout and Stress:** Automating repetitive and data-intensive tasks can significantly reduce the workload, stress, and potential for burnout among employees. This leads to a healthier work-life balance and a more sustainable work environment. Metrics could include tracking sick leave, stress-related incident reports, and overall employee well-being scores.

- **Increased Retention Rates:** When employees feel supported, valued, and equipped with modern tools, their likelihood of remaining with the organization increases. AI literacy is confirmed as a key variable linking positive personality traits (such as proactivity, openness to learning) and strong organizational support to overall work performance and job satisfaction. Organizations should track retention rates, particularly within teams that have actively embraced AI tools, and correlate these with measures of AI literacy and job satisfaction. This also includes assessing career progression and opportunities for skill development that arise from AI-driven efficiency.

- **Skill Development and Adaptability:** AI literacy encourages continuous learning and adaptability. Employees who embrace AI are often more inclined to develop new skills, which not only benefits their personal career growth but also strengthens the organization's overall talent pool and future readiness. This can be measured by participation rates in AI training programs and the acquisition of new, certified skills.

Leveraging AI to Measure AI Training Effectiveness

One of the most profound and transformative elements of a modern ROALI framework is the strategic deployment of AI itself to rigorously measure the success and impact of AI training initiatives. This creates a highly sophisticated and self-optimizing system where the technology that is being taught also becomes the arbiter of its own educational efficacy.[6]

AI-powered analytics offer a granular and insightful perspective on various facets of organizational development. These sophisticated tools can meticulously track changes in workforce productivity, identifying uplift or shifts directly attributable to the integration of new AI-driven skills. Beyond broad productivity metrics, AI can monitor individual employee learning progression through customized training modules, providing real-time insights into areas of strength and areas requiring further attention. Crucially, this extends to evaluating how effectively newly acquired skills—such as advanced prompting techniques for generative AI, data interpretation, or ethical AI considerations—are being applied on the job. This evaluation is performed against predefined, key business performance indicators (KPIs), ensuring that learning is directly tethered to tangible organizational objectives.

This inherent capability fosters the creation of a truly continuous and dynamic feedback loop. In this paradigm, AI not only delivers the training but also measures the efficacy of that very training. This leads to an iterative process of refinement and optimization, where both the content of the training and the desired learning outcomes are continuously improved. By meticulously linking the successful completion of customized training modules—for instance, achieving a high score on an Explainable AI (XAI) interpretation segment or demonstrating proficiency in a specific AI tool—directly to measurable business outcomes, organizations gain an unparalleled and scalable understanding of the true return on investment in corporate AI literacy. Such measurable outcomes could include a demonstrable reduction in compliance errors, a significant increase in decision-making speed and accuracy, enhanced customer satisfaction, or improved innovation rates. This comprehensive approach moves beyond anecdotal evidence, providing clear, data-driven validation of the strategic value and economic benefit derived from upskilling the workforce in AI capabilities.

Framework for Measuring Return on AI Literacy Investment (ROALI)

Measurement Category	Key Metrics	Targeted Improvement (Example)	Data Source
Efficiency & Productivity (Direct)	Average cycle time reduction for tasks, throughput rate increase, volume of tasks automated, average handling times	Operational efficiency increase (e.g., 53% improvement) due to effective prompt engineering	ERP workflow logs, collaboration suite usage reports (e.g., Copilot dashboard), time-tracking systems, ticketing system
Quality & Risk Mitigation (Direct)	Error rates in AI-assisted processes, compliance adherence score, reduction in AI-related security incidents (data exposure)	Reduction in errors requiring human correction; demonstrably sufficient AI literacy	Quality assurance audits, compliance monitoring tools, AI-SPM, and security logs
Strategic Value (Indirect)	Employee AI efficacy/ competence scores, innovation acceleration (number of new ideas/solutions), employee satisfaction and retention rates	Enhanced sense of control and competence in digital environments, shift toward value-driven, creative activities	Post-training assessments, sentiment analysis surveys, HRIS retention data, innovation pipeline tracking

The successful transition to an AI-augmented enterprise hinges critically on recognizing that AI literacy is the essential onramp to widespread production adoption. This necessitates a multifaceted approach that first addresses cultural anxieties and misconceptions surrounding AI, fostering an environment of acceptance and collaboration rather than fear of displacement. Following this, organizations must implement comprehensive, model-agnostic training programs that provide a foundational understanding of AI principles and applications. The crucial next step involves pivoting to highly specialized, role-based modules, ensuring that each employee, from data scientists to marketing professionals, understands how AI directly impacts their specific responsibilities and workflows. By systematically progressing through these stages, organizations can rapidly move from isolated pilot projects to scalable, enterprise-wide integration of AI solutions.

The strategic imperative demands that training must evolve significantly past generic Large Language Model (LLM) instructions, which often only scratch the surface of AI's potential. Instead, the focus must shift to advanced prompting techniques, such as Chain-of-Thought reasoning, which are vital for enhancing governance, ensuring ethical use, and achieving more accurate and reliable AI outputs. Furthermore, training must specifically address platform-specific usage within core collaboration suites (e.g., Microsoft 365, Google Workspace) and mission-critical systems (e.g., Enterprise Resource Planning [ERP], Human Resources Information Systems [HRIS], Customer Relationship Management [CRM]). This ensures that employees can seamlessly integrate AI tools into their daily operations, maximizing efficiency and minimizing disruption.

The necessity of customized and targeted training is further reinforced by growing regulatory pressures. For example, the EU AI Act's Article 4 explicitly mandates role-based competency in understanding and mitigating AI risks and upholding ethical principles. Organizations that proactively integrate training on Explainable AI (XAI) into functional workflows build the necessary trust that is paramount for successful AI adoption. By transforming AI models from opaque "black boxes" into transparent, auditable business partners, XAI fosters greater confidence among users and stakeholders, facilitating better decision-making and accountability.

Ultimately, continuous and strategic investment in AI literacy will determine an organization's long-term competitive vitality. This investment must be measured not merely by traditional return on investment but by a sophisticated Return on AI Literacy Investment framework. This framework quantifies broader strategic benefits, such as enhanced innovation, increased organizational agility, and improved decision-making, alongside more conventional operational efficiencies. The workforce must be empowered, not overwhelmed, by the rapid advancements in AI. By equipping human talent with the right skills, knowledge, and tools, organizations can unlock the full transformative potential of AI, driving sustained growth and competitive advantage in an increasingly AI-driven global economy.

CHAPTER 5

The Innovation Committee:
A Strategic Imperative for Enterprise AI

The establishment of a dedicated Innovation Committee (IC) is a mandatory requirement for any organization seeking to transition its artificial intelligence portfolio from a collection of unregulated experiments into integrated, trusted, and operational components within the enterprise. This structural framework is not merely a bureaucratic overhead; it serves as the indispensable foundation that underpins the safety, accountability, and strategic coherence of all AI initiatives. The successful realization of value from AI necessitates profound organizational transformation and successful change management, an effort that critically depends on proactive C-suite leadership and strategic direction.[1]

Effective AI governance fundamentally alters the strategic positioning of AI within a business. It provides the necessary rigor by mandating standards for explainability, auditability, and bias mitigation, which transforms novel technology into a sustainable competitive advantage. The primary barrier hindering the widespread deployment of cutting-edge technologies like Generative AI today is not technical failure but structural deficiency, specifically the lack of a robust governance model, coupled with significant risk and regulatory uncertainty, particularly for certain industries.

Organizations often struggle to achieve the desired ROI from their AI projects. This failure is frequently rooted in the inability to manage the associated risks effectively, causing projects to stall or fail regulatory review late in the development cycle. This not only leads to wasted resources but also erodes trust and diminishes the perceived value of AI initiatives within the organization. Therefore, the investment required to establish and staff a dedicated AI committee is not an overhead expense but a foundational capital expenditure necessary to secure the strategic value of all future AI investments. The committee's mandate must consequently be dual: to enable high-potential use cases by fostering innovation and exploration while simultaneously imposing the technical and ethical rigor necessary to ensure these projects successfully mature into trusted, compliant, and operationally sound components of the business. This holistic approach ensures that AI development is both agile and responsible, maximizing its potential while minimizing inherent risks.

The integration of an Innovation Committee into the early stages of AI development is not merely a procedural formality but a critical strategic justification designed to immediately mitigate what can be termed "compliance debt." This proactive approach underscores the fundamental principle that compliance must be intrinsically embedded into the foundational design and development stages of any AI initiative. This imperative begins as early as the Proof of Concept phase, setting a precedent for a governance-first mindset.

If compliance is relegated to an afterthought, treated as an attempt to retrofit regulatory requirements and ethical considerations post-development, organizations face a cascading series of massive and often prohibitive expenses. The arduous task of retroactively redesigning, re-engineering, and re-validating models and data pipelines to meet regulatory standards can easily exceed the initial implementation budget of the AI system itself. This "hidden cost" associated with belatedly addressing governance and compliance issues represents a significant financial drain that can cripple even the most promising AI projects.

Much like technical debt, which accrues interest and necessitates continuous effort and resources to resolve, regulatory debt carries an even graver risk: catastrophic legal and reputational complications. These complications can inevitably delay, or even completely derail, the production deployment of an AI system. The penalties for non-compliance, ranging from hefty fines to forced shutdowns and irreparable damage to public trust, far outweigh the initial investment in proactive governance.

By enforcing a rigorous compliance review at the earliest possible stage—specifically, Gate 1, which marks the Proof of Concept review—the IC assumes the critical function of a financial actuary. In this role, the committee preemptively identifies and mitigates future operational liabilities. This early intervention is instrumental in boosting the long-term financial viability and operational efficiency of an organization's AI production systems. It transforms compliance from a reactive burden into a strategic advantage, fostering trust, ensuring ethical AI deployment, and safeguarding the organization's reputation and financial health in an increasingly regulated and scrutinized technological landscape. This ensures that AI systems are not only innovative but also responsible, sustainable, and legally sound from their inception.

Defining the Committee's Core Charter and Mandate

The IC must be granted a clear and comprehensive mandate to establish, enforce, and continuously refine clear standards across critical ethical and technical dimensions. This mandate should explicitly cover explainability, ensuring that AI systems can articulate their reasoning and decision-making processes in an understandable manner. It must also encompass auditability, mandating that AI systems and their operations are transparent and can be systematically reviewed and verified. Finally, the mandate must address bias mitigation, requiring proactive measures to identify, assess, and reduce unfair biases in AI algorithms and data.

Operationally, the IC holds the paramount responsibility for providing strategic oversight and general guidance on all AI initiatives throughout the company. This expansive purview includes the approval and continuous oversight of all AI usage, whether at the individual employee level or across company-wide deployments. To foster institutional memory, ensure consistent decision-making, and promote best practices, the committee is tasked with mandating the creation and maintenance of a robust **AI Use Case Repository**. This repository will serve as the definitive historical reference for all AI initiatives, both those approved and those denied. For each entry, it must meticulously document associated risk assessments, detailing potential ethical, technical, and operational risks, along with the strategies for their mitigation. Crucially, the repository must also capture the rationale behind all final governance decisions, providing a transparent record of how and why specific AI projects were sanctioned or rejected. This systematic documentation is vital for learning from past experiences, adapting to new challenges, and maintaining a coherent and defensible AI strategy.

Recognizing that not all requests require the same level of scrutiny or adherence to a monthly meeting cadence, an expedited approval process can be established for minor requests or non-critical research into new technologies. These lower-risk approvals, which might involve explorations of nascent AI tools or preliminary investigations into new applications, can often be efficiently handled through direct email communication. This streamlined process would typically involve key leadership figures such as the Chief Executive Officer or Chief Technology Officer, in consultation with the Chief AI Officer, to ensure that even expedited approvals benefit from appropriate expertise and oversight without unduly delaying innovation.

Strategic Composition: Authority and Deep Expertise

The efficacy of the Innovation and Governance Committee is directly proportional to its cross-functional composition and, more importantly, the seniority of its members. The IGC must draw together key decision-makers and subject matter experts from a diverse range of departments to ensure every facet of AI risk—from technical failure to legal liability—is accounted for.

Governance and accountability are intrinsically tied to executive authority. Board directors and senior management stand at the forefront of AI accountability, where innovation intersects with legal, ethical, and reputational oversight. For an AI Governance, Risk, and Compliance (GRC) team to function effectively, securing executive support is considered a fundamental best practice.

A critical consideration in the formation of an effective AI oversight committee, such as an AI Steering Committee or similar governance body, is the seniority level of its membership. If the committee's composition is primarily drawn from roles below the Senior Vice President (SVP) or Vice President (VP) level, two significant and potentially debilitating structural problems are likely to emerge, severely hindering the committee's ability to fulfill its mandate.

Firstly, while individuals at lower management tiers may possess exceptional technical expertise and a deep understanding of the intricacies of AI development and implementation, they often lack the requisite positional authority to enforce difficult, cross-functional decisions. The nature of AI initiatives frequently necessitates actions that transcend individual departmental silos and may encounter resistance. For instance, an AI project might uncover the urgent need for a significant budget allocation toward retroactive data remediation to ensure the integrity and ethical use of data. Similarly, the committee might need to halt a high-profile but non-compliant project that was initiated by a peer department, even if that project has substantial internal backing. Without the positional authority inherent in SVP or VP roles, committee members may find themselves without the necessary leverage to compel compliance, demand resources, or overrule entrenched interests, thereby undermining the committee's ability to drive strategic change and mitigate risks effectively.

Secondly, and equally crucial, decision-makers for significant AI initiatives must possess the authority to allocate capital and scrutinize budgets comprehensively. AI projects, particularly those that are transformative or enterprise-wide, often require substantial financial investment, not only in technology and talent but also in infrastructure, data governance, and ongoing maintenance. By mandating SVP or VP-level representation on the committee, the organization ensures that "Go" decisions for AI projects are appropriately funded from the outset. This level of seniority guarantees that the necessary financial resources are committed, preventing promising initiatives from faltering due to insufficient capital. Conversely, it also ensures that "No-Go" decisions are binding and carry the weight of executive authority. This is vital for preventing the proliferation of unviable or non-strategic projects, optimizing resource allocation, and maintaining alignment between the overarching organizational AI strategy and the necessary capital allocation. Without this level of financial oversight and decision-making power, the committee risks becoming a mere advisory body, unable to translate its strategic recommendations into actionable and funded realities, thus jeopardizing the entire AI strategy of the organization.

Detailed Roles and Responsibilities

The required expertise must span the entire enterprise, with each function holding a specific, AI-native governance mandate:

- **AI Innovation Leader** (Chief Data Officer, VP Data, CAIO): Crucially, this function is the custodian of the AI Use Case Repository, serving as the designated expert and historian for all AI use cases within the organization. The AI leader bears significant responsibility for ensuring data provenance, upholding privacy standards, and guaranteeing the ethical use of AI. This encompasses a mandate to implement data minimization and anonymization techniques, thereby safeguarding consumer privacy. Furthermore, they are tasked with establishing and enforcing policies to ensure that the data used to train AI systems is representative, proactively mitigating the risk of bias propagation throughout the AI lifecycle. It is worth noting that in some organizational structures, these responsibilities might be bifurcated into two distinct roles.
- **IT Infrastructure & Enterprise Architecture** (CTO, VP of Infrastructure or Chief Enterprise Architect): This role manages the technical integration and physical infrastructure of AI systems. The VP must ensure the organization maintains a scalable architecture that can support the continuous, high-volume demands of production. The IT representative is mandated to ensure that the necessary MLOps (Machine Learning Operations) pipeline is in place to deliver model versioning, explainability logs, and real-time monitoring required for continuous auditability.

- **Security** (Chief Information Security Officer [CISO] or VP of Security): The CISO's mandate is to safeguard AI systems against cyber threats, data breaches, and adversarial attacks, which are common risks in the evolving digital landscape. This involves overseeing the integration of robust security measures, including adversarial testing, within the deployment pipeline. The Security lead manages third-party risk related to AI, protects against data poisoning, and leads the development of real-time monitoring capabilities necessary for the rapid detection of anomalous activity, ensuring prompt intervention and response.

- **Legal & Regulatory Affairs** (General Counsel or VP of Legal): The legal representative serves as the critical compliance gatekeeper. This individual reviews all Proofs of Concept against existing and emerging regulatory frameworks and is responsible for defining the minimum required level of model explainability needed for a system to be legally defensible in regulatory inquiries or court challenges. By mandating that AI systems be designed with regulatory demands in mind from the outset, the legal function prevents the accumulation of substantial "compliance debt." The mandate also extends to addressing intellectual property infringement and defining clear lines of accountability for AI outcomes.

- **Finance & Accounting** (VP of Financial Planning & Analysis, Controller, or CFO): The finance representative is tasked with assessing the economic viability and true ROI of all AI initiatives. This role rigorously scrutinizes budgets and capital allocation to ensure alignment with the AI strategy. The representative must also evaluate the often-hidden costs of governance and compliance that can otherwise exceed initial implementation budgets. Furthermore, the finance function is responsible for ensuring financial control assurance, which involves demanding that external controls reporting, such as SOC reports, be expanded to cover AI-specific risks related to models, data, and infrastructure.

- **Human Resources** (VP of HR or CHRO): The HR leader is tasked with addressing the ethical implications of AI on the workforce. This includes mitigating the risk of job displacement and managing unfair stereotypes or biases embedded in algorithmic systems, which can perpetuate unfairness in employment or financial opportunities. The HR representative is responsible for ensuring that internal AI systems, particularly those used for hiring or performance management, undergo rigorous additional checks for fairness and bias. Furthermore, the department facilitates ongoing AI ethics training for all staff and collaborates with the board to bridge any AI competence gaps within leadership.

- **Marketing & Public Relations** (VP of Marketing or Chief Brand Officer): This function is crucial for maintaining consumer trust and protecting the brand's reputation. The representative must develop and enforce clear policies governing AI deployment in marketing. This includes setting ethical boundaries against manipulative practices, such as deepfake advertising, and ensuring transparency by clearly labeling AI-generated content. The mandate is to prevent misinformation, manipulation of consumer behavior, and reputational damage stemming from biased or deceptive marketing content.

- **Sales** (VP Sales): The Vice President of Sales functions as both the commercial validator and the customer advocate for AI-powered products. Their principal responsibility is to ensure that all new innovations are not only marketable but also capable of being sold profitably at scale, and that their features directly address identified customer investment drivers. The sales VP provides data regarding areas where customers are actively seeking solutions, the extent of allocated budgets, and the specific features that influence deal closure or stagnation. This could assist in the prioritization of competing POC requests.

- **Product Leadership** (Chief Product Officer or VP of Product Development): The product leader plays a pivotal role in the strategic development and deployment of AI-powered products. This individual is responsible for ensuring that these products not only align with overarching business objectives but also demonstrably deliver significant customer value. A key area of ownership for the product leader is the strategic fit criteria within the innovation funnel, which dictates how new AI initiatives are prioritized and advanced. The product leader must champion a user-centric design philosophy for all AI systems. This involves incorporating features that prioritize user autonomy and transparency. Examples of such features include clear transparency statements that explain how AI decisions are made, and robust mechanisms for users to appeal or opt out of AI-driven decisions. These elements are essential for building trust and preserving user control in an increasingly AI-driven landscape.

Cross-Functional Committee Composition and Mandates

Department/ Role	Required Seniority (Decision Maker)	Primary AI Governance Mandate	Critical Risk Focus
IT Infrastructure/ EA	VP / Chief Enterprise Architect / CTO	Technical integration, MLOps, use case history	Scalability, system failure, version control
Security	CISO / VP of Security	Adversarial testing, real-time threat monitoring	Data breach, data poisoning, unauthorized access
Legal & Regulatory	General Counsel / VP of Legal	Compliance, IP/ contractual liability, defensibility	Regulatory penalties, IP infringement, compliance debt
Finance & Accounting	VP of FP&A / CFO Rep	ROI modeling, budget allocation, hidden cost forecasting	Financial viability, cost overruns, control gaps

Department/ Role	Required Seniority (Decision Maker)	Primary AI Governance Mandate	Critical Risk Focus
Human Resources	VP of Workforce Strategy	Ethical employment, internal bias audits, leadership fluency	Discrimination, workforce disruption, skills gap
Marketing	VP of Marketing / CBO	Ethical communication, consumer trust, transparency	Reputational damage, manipulation, misinformation/ deepfakes
Product Leadership	Chief Product Officer / VP of Product	Strategic alignment, customer experience, user rights	Market misalignment, feature ethicality, user autonomy
AI	Chief Data Officer / Chief AI Officer	Data quality, provenance, privacy, model training sets	Bias propagation, privacy violations, data adequacy

The composition of the leadership committee is a critical factor and may vary considerably based on the organization's unique structure and strategic imperatives. For instance, in companies that operate with a decentralized model, it is common to find multiple product leaders serving on the committee. Each of these leaders contributes their specific domain expertise, thereby enriching the strategic oversight of AI product development. This multifaceted approach is instrumental in enhancing both the breadth and depth of strategic guidance provided for AI initiatives, ensuring a comprehensive and well-rounded perspective.

To ensure efficient decision-making and avoid stalemates, the committee should ideally be composed of an odd number of members. A recommended size would fall somewhere between 9 and 13 individuals, striking a balance between diverse representation and agile operations. The larger end of this spectrum, closer to 13, is particularly relevant for companies that manage multiple distinct product lines or operate across various industries, requiring a broader range of insights. In some organizational contexts, roles might be more finely granular, leading to the inclusion of specialized positions such as a Chief AI Officer, a Chief Data Officer, and a Chief Technology Officer. Each of these roles brings distinct and invaluable expertise to the table, further strengthening the committee's ability to navigate the complex landscape of AI strategy and implementation. The Chief AI Officer, for example, would focus on the overarching AI vision and ethical considerations, while the Chief Data Officer would ensure data governance and quality, and the Chief Technology Officer would oversee the technological infrastructure and integration.

Operational Cadence and Communication Flow

For organizations deeply entrenched in significant AI transformation and rapid deployment, a monthly meeting cadence is not merely optimal but essential. This frequent interaction is critical in complex data environments to effectively manage the high velocity of new ideas, POCs, and regulatory changes, thereby preventing the accumulation of a debilitating backlog.

In less data-intensive sectors, organizations with highly stable AI portfolios, or those just initiating AI programs, might find a quarterly meeting schedule to be an acceptable minimum. Defaulting to an ad-hoc or "as-needed" basis carries substantial risks. Such an unstructured approach invariably invites governance lapses, compromises data quality, and elevates compliance risks, all of which contribute to a significant slowdown in innovation.

Therefore, it is imperative that the innovation leader—whether holding the title of Chief AI Officer (CAIO), Chief Data Officer (CDO), or Chief Technology Officer (CTO)—enforces a structured, monthly meeting cadence. This consistent oversight is fundamental to maintaining continuous visibility into AI initiatives, ensuring alignment with strategic objectives, and proactively addressing emergent challenges and opportunities within the dynamic AI landscape. Regular, scheduled discussions facilitate prompt decision-making, foster cross-functional collaboration, and reinforce accountability, all of which are vital for sustained success and responsible growth in AI.

The IC meeting agenda must be structured to ensure balance between long-term strategic oversight and urgent operational review.

Operational Review (Monthly Focus): The monthly operational cadence is meticulously designed to provide a comprehensive overview of immediate project flow and performance data for AI initiatives. This structured approach ensures agile decision-making and proactive risk management.

Key agenda items for these critical monthly meetings include:

- **Review and Decision on New AI Proofs of Concept (POCs):** This segment is dedicated to evaluating all newly proposed AI Proofs of Concept. Each POC undergoes a rigorous assessment, considering its strategic alignment, technical feasibility, potential business impact, required resources, and estimated return on investment. A collaborative discussion among stakeholders culminates in a formal decision for either approval or rejection, ensuring that only viable and value-driven projects proceed to the next stage of development. This step is crucial for maintaining a focused and effective AI development pipeline. Prior to the meeting various preliminary assessments should be accomplished, including but not limited to (1) any security assessment for new products or services, (2) resource availability for supporting teams (i.e., operation, data, security, development), and (3) alignment with corporate strategy.

- **Detailed Review of Continuous Monitoring Reports:** A substantial portion of the meeting is allocated to an in-depth examination of continuous monitoring reports for all active AI initiatives. This review is critical for understanding the real-time health and performance of deployed AI systems. Specific metrics that are meticulously analyzed include:

- » **Model Drift:** Assessing how significantly the model's predictions have deviated from expected performance over time, often due to changes in input data distribution.
- » **Bias Indices:** Evaluating any emerging or persistent biases within the model's outputs, ensuring fairness and ethical AI implementation.
- » **Budget Alignment:** Tracking the financial performance of AI projects against allocated budgets, identifying any overruns or efficiencies.
- » **Performance Degradation:** Monitoring for any decline in the model's accuracy, precision, recall, or other relevant performance indicators, which could signal underlying issues requiring intervention. This detailed analysis allows for the timely identification of anomalies and the initiation of corrective actions to maintain optimal model performance and reliability.

- **Review of Recent High-Risk Incidents and Escalations:** This agenda item focuses on a thorough post-mortem analysis of all recent high-risk incidents and escalations related to AI operations. The objective is twofold:
  - » **Root Cause Analysis:** To systematically identify the underlying causes of each incident, moving beyond surface-level symptoms to understand fundamental issues. This often involves reviewing logs, studying incident reports, and conducting interviews with relevant personnel.
  - » **Assessment of Escalation Protocol Effectiveness:** To evaluate how well established escalation protocols functioned during the incident. This includes assessing the clarity of communication channels, the speed of response, the adequacy of resource allocation, and the ultimate resolution of the issue. The insights gained from this review are instrumental in refining existing processes, enhancing incident response strategies, and strengthening the overall resilience and robustness of the AI production framework.

Strategic Review (Quarterly Focus): These critical sessions are designed for high-level directional setting, ensuring the organization's AI initiatives remain strategically aligned and effectively managed. Key agenda items for these meetings should include a thorough review of the AI Use Case Repository, providing an opportunity to assess the current portfolio of AI applications and identify areas for optimization or expansion.

Furthermore, these sessions are essential for evaluating the overall strategic direction of the AI portfolio, ensuring it aligns with the organization's broader business objectives and market demands. This involves a comprehensive analysis of the existing AI strategy, identifying potential gaps and formulating adjustments to capitalize on emerging opportunities.

A crucial component of these meetings is the review of findings from any external audits. This allows for an independent assessment of the organization's AI practices, identifying potential risks, compliance issues, or areas for improvement in data governance, ethical considerations, and model performance. The insights gleaned from these audits are vital for maintaining responsible and secure AI deployment.

Discussions around necessary updates based on emerging regulatory changes are also paramount. The landscape of AI regulation is constantly evolving, and these sessions provide a forum to understand the implications of new laws and guidelines on the organization's AI operations. Proactive adaptation to these changes is critical for ensuring legal compliance and mitigating reputational risks.

Finally, and of utmost importance, it is critical that these meetings include specific time dedicated to leadership AI fluency training and updates. Given the transformative nature of AI, board and C-suite knowledge of AI risk and opportunity is absolutely essential for effective oversight. This training should encompass an understanding of AI fundamentals, potential ethical implications, data privacy concerns, and the strategic advantages AI can offer. By fostering a well-informed leadership team, the organization can make sound decisions regarding AI investment, development, and deployment, ultimately driving innovation and sustainable growth while managing inherent risks.

To maintain agility and prevent the IC meeting cycle from impeding progress, it is crucial to establish clear and efficient protocols for making decisions outside of regularly scheduled meetings. For initiatives categorized as low-risk, or for requests that involve further investigation into particular technologies or past committee decisions, a streamlined approval process can be implemented.

Specifically, such non-critical matters can be swiftly approved through direct email communication between the Chief Technology Officer and the Chief AI Officer. This rapid communication channel ensures that decisions on these items are made quickly, preventing them from becoming bottlenecks and significantly improving the overall velocity of these projects. This approach allows the organization to remain responsive and agile, addressing minor issues and research requests without the need to wait for a formal committee meeting. All off-cycle projects are included in the AI Use Case Repository and tracked in future IC monthly meetings.

The Enterprise Innovation Funnel: From Idea to POC Gateway

The IC acts as a series of crucial phase gates within the organization's innovation funnel—the systematic process used to filter raw ideas into actionable, high-potential solutions. By integrating governance checkpoints into this funnel, the organization ensures that only the best ideas—those with strong business rationale, technical feasibility, and confirmed compliance—are allowed to proceed.

Stage 1: Broad-Spectrum Ideation and Strategic Vetting

The initial stage, often referred to as the **Ideation and Vision Alignment Phase**, is critical for establishing a strong foundation for any new initiative or product development. This phase is characterized by a deliberate and expansive effort to collect a wide and diverse range of ideas. These ideas are not limited to a single source but are actively sought from a broad spectrum of contributors, including:

- **Employees:** Internal talent, with their unique perspectives and understanding of operational intricacies, can offer valuable insights and innovative solutions. Their direct experience with existing processes and customer interactions often fuels practical and implementable ideas.

- **Customers:** As the ultimate end-users, customers provide invaluable feedback and articulate their needs, pain points, and desires. Market research, surveys, focus groups, and direct feedback channels are essential for capturing these perspectives. Understanding customer needs is paramount to developing solutions that genuinely resonate with the target audience.
- **Stakeholders:** This broad category includes investors, partners, suppliers, and even regulatory bodies. Their input ensures that ideas not only are innovative but also align with broader business objectives, market realities, and ethical considerations.

This robust collection of ideas is frequently fueled and informed by three key drivers:

- **Market Trend Analysis:** A thorough examination of current and emerging market trends helps identify opportunities and potential areas for innovation. This includes analyzing technological advancements, shifting consumer behaviors, competitive landscapes, and economic indicators. Understanding these trends allows the organization to anticipate future demands and position itself strategically.
- **Customer Needs Research:** Beyond simply collecting ideas, deep-dive research into customer needs, both stated and unstated, is crucial. This involves understanding their motivations, challenges, and aspirations, which can reveal unmet needs that present significant opportunities for new products or services.
- **Internal Efficiencies:** A significant portion of employees will dedicate their efforts to this crucial driver. Their primary objective will be to identify and propose solutions for enhancing internal efficiencies within the organization. This involves a proactive approach to scrutinizing existing workflows, identifying bottlenecks, and suggesting innovative methods for improvement or automation of manual processes. Examples include process

optimization, technology adoption, workflow automation, and knowledge management.

A central figure in this stage is the **Chief Innovation and Alignment Officer (CIAO)**, or a similar leadership role responsible for innovation strategy. The CIAO's primary responsibility during this phase is to act as a guardian of the organization's overarching vision. This involves:

- **Ensuring Vision Guidance:** The CIAO must ensure that all ideation efforts are consciously guided by the organization's long-term vision, mission, and strategic objectives. This prevents the ideation process from becoming a disconnected exercise and keeps it focused on contributing to the company's ultimate goals.
- **Preliminary Alignment Check:** While not a stage for rigorous vetting, the CIAO conducts a preliminary check for alignment with strategic goals. This ensures that the generated ideas, even in their nascent form, bear some relevance to the organization's strategic direction. This initial filtering is light-touch but crucial for preventing significant deviations later on.

At this juncture, the overarching focus is deliberately placed on quantity and diversity rather than immediate feasibility or detailed evaluation. The goal is to cast a wide net, encourage out-of-the-box thinking, and gather as many varied ideas as possible. This approach fosters a culture of innovation and ensures that a broad spectrum of possibilities is explored. Consequently, risk filtering is minimal at this initial stage. Excessive scrutiny or premature elimination of ideas can stifle creativity and prevent potentially groundbreaking concepts from emerging. The emphasis is on open-mindedness and the belief that even seemingly impractical ideas can contain the seed of a revolutionary solution. The detailed analysis and risk assessment will come in subsequent stages, after a robust pool of diverse ideas has been established.

To facilitate this stage, a simple digital form with key information helps to streamline the process.

AI Project Ideation Form

Section 1: The Idea & Business Opportunity (The "Why")

1. **Project Title & Origin:**

   » **Title:** A concise, descriptive name (e.g., "AI-Powered Churn Prediction Model").
   » **Proposer/Department:** Name of the person or team submitting the idea.
   » **Idea Source:** e.g., Customer Feedback, Competitive Analysis, Internal Efficiency Need, New Technology Capability.

2. **Problem Statement (The Pain Point):**

   » What specific, measurable problem does this AI project solve (e.g., "Our current manual document review process leads to a 3-week delay in client onboarding")?

3. **Target Outcome & Value Proposition:**

   » What is the proposed solution (in plain language)?
   » What is the **measurable business value** if successful (e.g., "Reduce onboarding time by 50%," or "Increase lead conversion rate by 10%")?
   » *Sales/Marketing Relevance:* How does this innovation generate new revenue or protect existing revenue?

Section 2: Technical Approach & Feasibility (The "How")

4. **AI/ML Technique Proposed:**

   » What type of AI/ML are you proposing (e.g., Generative AI/ LLM, Predictive Analytics/Forecasting, Computer Vision, Classification)?
   » Will this use an existing product in a new way?
   » Are you looking at an additional off-the-shelf product to assist?

5. **Data Requirements:**

   » What core data sets are needed to train and run this model (e.g., Historical Sales Data, Customer Service Transcripts, Product Usage Logs)?
   » Is the required data already available (Yes/No/Partial)?
   » Is the data clean/labeled/structured?

6. **Technical Feasibility (Initial Assessment):**

   » Is this technically possible with current resources/technology?
   » Estimated complexity (Low/Medium/High).

Section 3: Compliance, Ethics, & Resource (The "Guardrails")

7. **Ethical & Reputational Risk Screening (Marketing/Legal Input):**

   » Will this AI directly interact with customers (Yes/No)?
   » Does this project involve creating synthetic content (e.g., voice, text, images, video)?
   » Transparency: How will the user be informed they are interacting with AI (labeling/disclosure)?
   » Bias/Fairness: Which demographic groups could be negatively impacted by model bias?

8. **Data & Privacy Compliance (Legal/CISO Input):**

   » Does the project use Personally Identifiable Information (PII) or confidential client data (Yes/No)?
   » What regulatory constraints apply (e.g., GDPR, HIPAA, internal policy)?

9. **Estimated Resource Needs (Initial):**

   » Estimated Team/Skills (e.g., 1 Data Scientist, 1 Engineer, 0.5 Project Manager).
   » Estimated Timeline for Proof of Concept (e.g., 3 months).

Section 4: Next Steps

10. **Proposal Rating (Committee Use Only):**

   » Strategic Alignment (1–5).
   » Feasibility (1–5).
   » Risk Level (Low/Medium/High).

Stage 2: Concept Development and Preliminary Business Case Construction

In this foundational stage of project development, nascent ideas undergo a crucial transformation into well-defined, actionable concepts. Concurrently, preliminary business cases are meticulously constructed to assess the potential of these concepts. The paramount objective of this initial phase gate is to act as a robust filter, efficiently identifying and discarding projects that demonstrate inherent weaknesses early in their lifecycle. This proactive approach is critical for preventing the misallocation of valuable resources—be it financial, human, or technological—to concepts that ultimately prove to be technically unfeasible or lacking clear, demonstrable market demand.

The criteria employed for this initial filtering process are multifaceted and strategically aligned with overarching organizational goals. Typically, these criteria encompass:

- **Financial Viability:** This involves a preliminary assessment of whether the estimated budget for a project aligns with the organization's financial capacity and strategic investment priorities. Projects with exorbitant costs relative to their potential return or those that significantly exceed established budgetary guidelines are flagged for further scrutiny or early rejection.
- **Market Demand:** A thorough, albeit preliminary, understanding of the target market is essential. This includes evaluating the existence of a genuine need or desire for the proposed solution, the size and growth potential of the market, and the competitive landscape. Projects addressing niche markets with limited growth prospects or those entering saturated markets without a clear competitive advantage may not pass this filter.

- **Security Review:** During this crucial phase, preliminary review by the cybersecurity office is mandatory. This review must encompass all proposed technologies, software solutions, and data integration methods known at this time. The cybersecurity office will assess potential vulnerabilities, and ensure compliance with established security protocols and regulatory requirements. This proactive measure is essential to mitigate risks, maintain data integrity, and safeguard the organization's digital assets.
- **Resource Availability:** This criterion assesses whether the organization possesses the necessary human capital, technological infrastructure, and other critical resources to successfully execute the project. A concept, no matter how promising, cannot advance if the requisite expertise or tools are unavailable or cannot be procured within a reasonable timeframe and budget.

Cross-functional teams, comprising experts from various departments such as R&D, marketing, finance, security, and operations, play a pivotal role in this stage. They collaborate using a systematic and standardized approach to evaluate and prioritize projects. This collaborative effort ensures that only those projects that demonstrably align with the organization's strategic objectives and long-term vision are put forward. This rigorous internal vetting process ensures that by the time projects are submitted for a more comprehensive and formal review, they have already undergone a significant level of scrutiny and have a solid preliminary foundation, increasing their chances of securing further investment and development.

Stage 3: The Proof of Concept Phase as the Compliance Integration Point

Once a proposal successfully navigates the initial two stages of review, it is then presented to the full Innovation Committee for comprehensive evaluation. This pivotal moment is where the committee casts its vote on whether to advance the project into the Proof of Concept phase. The POC stage represents the most critical juncture for the IC, as it serves as the mandatory point for integrating all necessary security, compliance, and regulatory requirements. This proactive approach ensures that compliance is meticulously built directly into the system's fundamental design, thereby preventing the catastrophic and often costly necessity of retrofitting these essential elements at a later, more advanced stage of development.

The IC assumes the crucial role of strategic gatekeeper, meticulously and rigorously reviewing all proposed POCs against a formalized and comprehensive risk register. This register extends far beyond conventional technical or financial feasibility assessments, delving deeply into non-negotiable ethical concerns. These include, but are not limited to, the potential risk of generating false or misleading content (often referred to as "hallucinations" in AI contexts) and the presence of embedded biases that could inadvertently lead to unfair, discriminatory, or otherwise unintended consequences. This proactive, front-loaded approach to risk mitigation is designed to prevent major legal and ethical complications that frequently arise in later stages, often causing significant delays or even completely derailing a project's production deployment. By addressing these critical issues early on, the IC safeguards the organization from reputational damage, legal liabilities, and the immense financial and operational costs associated with late-stage remediation.

Stage 4: Rigorous Decision-Making: The AI Go/No-Go Matrix and Risk Register

To execute its strategic gating function, the IC must rely on structured, objective decision-making tools. The primary mechanism is the phase-gate process, which uses a systematic Go/No-Go decision matrix tied directly to a comprehensive AI risk register.

The decision-making process is structured to rigorously evaluate ideas at the conclusion of each developmental stage. This systematic approach ensures that only those concepts demonstrating the most compelling business rationale, a strong customer-centric focus, and robust technical viability are granted approval to proceed and consume additional resources.

Central to this evaluation is the AI risk register, a dynamic document that plays a critical role in proactive risk management. This register serves to:

- **Identify Potential Roadblocks:** It meticulously lists and describes any foreseeable challenges or obstacles that could impede the project's progress.
- **Estimate Likelihood and Impact:** For each identified risk, the register quantifies the probability of its occurrence and assesses the potential severity of its consequences if it materializes.
- **Outline Tangible Mitigation Measures:** Crucially, it prescribes clear, actionable strategies and steps designed to either prevent risks from occurring, reduce their likelihood, or minimize their impact should they arise.

For initiatives involving AI, the risk register requires an expanded scope. Beyond the standard project risks (e.g., budget overruns, technical challenges, resource allocation issues), it must explicitly track ethical and compliance risks. This includes, but is not limited to, considerations such as:

- **Bias in AI Models:** potential for algorithms to perpetuate or amplify existing societal biases, leading to unfair or discriminatory outcomes
- **Data Privacy and Security:** risks associated with the collection, storage, processing, and use of sensitive data by AI systems, ensuring adherence to regulations like GDPR or CCPA
- **Transparency and Explainability:** challenges in understanding how AI models arrive at their decisions, particularly in critical applications, and the need for clear communication of their limitations
- **Accountability:** establishing clear lines of responsibility for AI system performance, failures, and unintended consequences
- **Regulatory Compliance:** adherence to evolving laws and industry standards related to AI development and deployment, including ethical guidelines and specific sector regulations

By integrating these critical ethical and compliance considerations directly into the risk register, organizations can ensure a more holistic and responsible approach to AI development, safeguarding against reputational damage, legal penalties, and a loss of public trust, while simultaneously advancing innovative solutions.

Beyond conventional evaluation metrics such as market demand and financial viability, the Innovation Committee must incorporate a set of mandatory, scored criteria explicitly centered on core governance pillars for AI projects. These criteria are designed to quantify ethical and compliance requirements, elevating them to the status of measurable technical specifications rather than treating them as optional philosophical considerations. This approach ensures that responsible AI practices are embedded throughout the project lifecycle and are subject to the same rigorous scrutiny as technical performance.

Key governance pillars for AI project assessment are as follows:

- **Bias Mitigation (Fairness Policies):** The committee's assessment must thoroughly scrutinize the representativeness of the training data used for the AI model. It is imperative to evaluate whether proactive strategies have been implemented to actively reduce or eliminate biases that could lead to discriminatory outcomes. This includes a comprehensive evaluation of the model against established fairness indices, ensuring adherence to organizational and regulatory policies explicitly designed to prevent discrimination across various protected characteristics. Projects should detail the methodologies used for bias detection (e.g., disparate impact analysis, subgroup analysis) and the specific techniques employed for mitigation (e.g., re-sampling, re-weighting, adversarial de-biasing).

- **Explainability (Transparency Statements):** This criterion is crucial for assessing the transparency and interpretability of the AI system's decision-making process for human stakeholders. For decisions with significant impact—such as those in critical sectors like finance, human resources, or healthcare—a low degree of explainability must unequivocally result in a "No-Go" decision for the project. Projects are required to include concrete plans for the publication of AI disclosures or "fact sheets." These documents should concisely summarize the system's core functionalities, its underlying logic, and, critically, its limitations, thereby fostering trust and accountability. Evaluation should consider the chosen explainability methods (e.g., LIME, SHAP, counterfactual explanations) and their appropriateness for the specific application.

- **Auditability and Traceability:** The IC must meticulously verify that robust mechanisms are in place for systematically reviewing and verifying the performance, data inputs, and outputs of all AI systems. This necessitates ironclad assurance that the MLOps pipeline unequivocally guarantees comprehensive model versioning, allowing for the tracking of all changes and iterations, and meticulous compliance logging, ensuring a complete and unalterable record of all relevant actions and decisions. This pillar is essential for post-deployment monitoring, regulatory compliance, and retrospective analysis of system behavior.

- **Hallucination and Accuracy:** Specifically for generative AI models, the committee is responsible for defining the acceptable error rate for the generation of false, misleading, or nonsensical content—commonly referred to as hallucinations. This demands documented adversarial testing, a rigorous process designed to stress-test the model against anticipated failure modes and identify vulnerabilities where it might produce inaccurate or fabricated information. Projects must present the results of these tests and outline strategies for minimizing hallucination, such as employing robust data grounding techniques and confidence scoring.

- **Recourse and Appeal:** The AI system must incorporate clear and accessible user interaction protocols. This critically includes the establishment of effective mechanisms that empower users to contest AI-driven decisions and, when appropriate, request human review or intervention. This not only builds essential consumer trust by providing avenues for redress but also ensures unwavering adherence to fundamental consumer rights and legal frameworks regarding automated decision-making. Projects should outline the user interface for appeals, the expected response times for human review, and the process for resolving contested decisions.

AI Proof of Concept Go/No-Go Evaluation Matrix

Criteria Category	Specific Metric / Question	Depart-mental Owner	Scoring Weight (Scale 1–5)	Go Threshold Requirement (Minimum Score)
Regulatory & Compliance	Full alignment with required data privacy laws (GDPR, CCPA, etc.)?	Legal/ Security	5	Must meet 5/5 (non-negotiable)
Compliance Debt Risk	Is compliance embedded from design, or will retrofitting be required?	Finance/ Legal	4	Score must be 4 or higher (proactive compliance)
Bias Mitigation	Model tested against fairness indices (e.g., disparate impact) with results acceptable to HR?	HR/Data Science	5	Must meet 4/5 (demonstrated mitigation efforts)
Model Explainability	Is the model transparent enough for the decision context (high-stakes decisions require high explainability)?	Product/ Data Science	3	Varies by context, minimum 3/5

Criteria Category	Specific Metric / Question	Depart-mental Owner	Scoring Weight (Scale 1–5)	Go Threshold Requirement (Minimum Score)
Hallucination Risk	Defined error/false content generation rate meets operational acceptance threshold? (Requires adversarial testing)	Security/IT	4	Must meet 4/5 (acceptable risk)
User Recourse	Does the system include an immediate human oversight/appeal mechanism?	Product	3	Must meet 3/5 (trust building)
Technical Viability (MLOps Readiness)	Is the MLOps infrastructure (monitoring, versioning, audit logging) in place for continuous governance?	IT Infra-structure	4	Must meet 4/5

Continuous Governance and MLOps Integration

Governance in the realm of AI is not a static checkpoint but a dynamic, continuous process deeply embedded within daily workflows and operational structures. This unwavering vigilance is paramount for fostering and maintaining trust in AI systems while simultaneously adapting to the ever-evolving landscape of AI-related risks. The initial deployment of an AI model marks not an end but the beginning of a continuous oversight journey.

The critical link between high-level executive policy (governance) and the intricate technical realities of AI implementation is Machine Learning Operations. MLOps provides a robust and structured framework for comprehensively managing AI models throughout their entire lifecycle. This framework ensures that models remain consistently compliant, accountable, and secure from development through deployment and beyond. Without this essential technical infrastructure, even the most well-intentioned governance policies become practically unenforceable, thereby creating significant compliance liabilities and exposing organizations to undue risk.

MLOps delivers several key functionalities that are indispensable for effective and continuous AI governance:

- **Continuous Monitoring:** MLOps workflows are designed to actively track and identify data drift and concept drift. Data drift occurs when the characteristics of real-world input data diverge from the data used to train the model, while concept drift signifies a change in the relationship between the input and output variables. Real-time tracking of these drifts is crucial for aligning model accuracy with current conditions and preventing performance degradation, thereby ensuring consistent and reliable output from AI systems.

- **Compliance Audits & Logging:** MLOps plays a vital role in maintaining comprehensive Model Versioning and Explainability Logs. This capability automates the meticulous recording of AI decision-making processes, providing an auditable trail that is essential for regulatory reporting and compliance audits. These logs offer transparency into how and why an AI model reached a particular decision, which is critical for accountability.

- **Automated Bias Detection:** To mitigate ethical risks, MLOps enables continuous model audits and integrates real-time bias detection tools. These capabilities are crucial for proactively identifying and preventing the unintended introduction or amplification of biases within production models over time. This continuous scrutiny ensures fairness and equitable outcomes from AI systems.

It is imperative that the budget allocated to MLOps infrastructure be recognized by the IC not merely as an operational IT cost but as a fundamental governance cost. MLOps is the singular mechanism that renders the ethical policies established by the committee technically defensible and auditable. Investing in MLOps is, therefore, an investment in the integrity, trustworthiness, and long-term viability of an organization's AI strategy.

Effective AI governance hinges on a robust framework that transforms raw operational data into actionable insights for strategic decision-making. This process ensures that AI systems not only perform optimally but also adhere to ethical guidelines and regulatory standards. The MLOps pipeline, a critical component of this framework, generates extensive telemetry data, which must be meticulously synthesized into executive-level reports for the IC. These reports serve as the foundation for the IC's oversight, enabling them to trigger necessary human interventions, such as manual model adjustments or retraining, or to initiate automated retraining processes when predefined thresholds are breached.

To maintain transparency, accountability, and continuous improvement in AI systems, the following essential governance metrics are crucial for reporting to the IC:

- **Risk Metric: Model Drift (Data or Concept)**
    - » **Description:** This metric quantifies deviations in model performance due to changes in the underlying data distribution (data drift) or the relationship between input and output variables (concept drift). Both types of drift can significantly degrade model accuracy and reliability over time.
    - » **Operational Thresholds:** Clearly defined operational thresholds are essential for flagging significant drift. For instance, a predefined operational threshold of a 5% performance dip (e.g., a 5% reduction in accuracy, precision, or recall) serves as a critical trigger for immediate investigation and intervention.[1] Exceeding this threshold indicates a strong likelihood that the model is no longer performing as intended and requires attention.

- » **Reporting Focus:** Reports should detail the specific type of drift detected, the magnitude of the performance degradation, the potential root causes (e.g., changes in user behavior, seasonal trends, data pipeline issues), and the proposed mitigation strategies.

- **Fairness Metric: Measurable Shift in Fairness Index**
  - » **Description:** This metric assesses the equitable performance of AI models across different demographic subgroups. AI systems, if not carefully designed and monitored, can inadvertently perpetuate or amplify existing biases present in training data, leading to unfair or discriminatory outcomes for certain groups. The Fairness Index, a composite metric, quantifies the degree of fairness based on predefined criteria (e.g., equal opportunity, demographic parity, predictive parity).
  - » **Bias Creep Detection:** Any measurable shift in the calculated Fairness Index for specific demographic subgroups, even seemingly minor fluctuations, is a critical indicator of potential bias creep. This necessitates immediate attention to prevent the entrenchment of discriminatory practices.
  - » **Mandatory Retraining or Mitigation:** Upon detection of a significant shift, mandatory retraining of the model with debiased data, implementation of fairness-aware algorithms, or other targeted mitigation strategies are imperative to restore equitable performance and ensure ethical AI deployment. Reporting should detail the affected subgroups, the nature of the bias, and the specific actions taken to address it.

- **Compliance Metric: Adherence to Ethical and Regulatory Standards**
  - » **Description:** This metric evaluates the AI system's adherence to internal ethical guidelines, industry best practices, and external regulatory requirements. It encompasses a broad range of indicators that reflect the organization's commitment to responsible AI development and deployment.

- » **Key Performance Indicators (KPIs):**
  - O **Percentage of AI Tools Reviewed by the Ethics Committee Before Launch:** This KPI measures the proactive engagement of the Ethics Committee in the AI development lifecycle. A high percentage indicates a strong commitment to ethical considerations from the initial stages of development. It ensures that potential ethical risks are identified and addressed before deployment.
  - O **Time Required to Resolve AI-Related Compliance Issues:** This KPI measures the efficiency and effectiveness of the organization's response to identified compliance breaches or ethical concerns. A short resolution time indicates a robust incident response framework and a proactive approach to maintaining compliance.

- » **Reporting Focus:** Reports should provide an overview of compliance status, highlight any areas of non-compliance, detail the actions taken to rectify issues, and outline strategies for continuous improvement in ethical and regulatory adherence.

The diligent application and reporting of these metrics are paramount for ensuring that operational performance is continuously traced back to its origins. This traceability allows organizations to understand the underlying factors influencing AI behavior and to quickly identify and address any anomalies. Furthermore, these metrics ensure that all AI outputs are defensible in terms of their ethical implications, accuracy, and adherence to established standards. By prioritizing robust governance and continuous monitoring, organizations can build trust in their AI systems, mitigate risks, and unlock the full potential of artificial intelligence responsibly.

Continuous governance of AI systems is fundamentally dependent on the establishment and consistent application of clear, rigorous escalation protocols. These protocols serve as the essential operational framework for promptly identifying, accurately assessing, and effectively addressing emergent issues, risks, regulatory requirements, and performance deviations across the entire AI lifecycle.

The Escalation Path:

1. **Risk Monitoring Systems:** The process begins with automated systems (MLOps, AI-driven real-time threat monitoring) detecting anomalies—such as unusual login behavior, data movement, or a sudden bias shift—and generating intelligent alerts.

2. **Tier 1 Response:** Designated functional teams (Data Science, Security Operations) conduct immediate, internal triage and analysis.

3. **Tier 2 Escalation (Committee Notification):** If the issue is categorized as medium or high risk (e.g., a critical security failure, a high-profile bias incident, or sustained performance degradation), it must be escalated immediately to the committee chairs (CTO, General Counsel) via a standardized communication framework.

4. **Tier 3 Intervention (Committee Action):** The IGC reviews the issue and mandates corrective action, which may range from manual human override of the AI decision, rapid automated retraining, or, in extreme cases, temporary system shutdown.

As with other technology infrastructure, the committee must regularly test and simulate these escalation paths to ensure operational readiness, much like running a fire drill. This practice enhances trust among stakeholders by demonstrating accountability and prepares the organization for immediate action should a critical failure occur.

The formation and launch of the AI Innovation Committee represents a critical shift from viewing AI as an optional technological experiment to integrating it as a vital, accountable component of enterprise operations. The CAIO's mandate in launching this committee is to enforce structure, specifically cross-functional senior leadership, a mandatory monthly operational cadence, and a rigorous, quantified Go/No-Go decision matrix, a critical step in a company's AI maturity. By embedding compliance into the Proof of Concept phase and leveraging the MLOps pipeline for continuous, real-time monitoring, the organization proactively avoids crippling "compliance debt" and ensures that ethical standards (explainability, auditability, bias mitigation) are maintained throughout the entire AI lifecycle. This integrated, continuous governance framework is the single most critical structural element required to translate technological promise into sustainable, trustworthy, and high-ROI business transformation.

CHAPTER 6

Pillar Five:
Annually Funding the POC Pipeline with a Dedicated Budget

The successful progression of AI from experimental POC to reliable, scaled production requires a fundamental re-evaluation of organizational funding strategies. Historically, innovation has been financed through short-term operational expenditures (OpEx), a model fundamentally incompatible with the long-term, asset-intensive nature of AI deployment. To truly harness AI's transformative potential, organizations must establish predictable, sustained financial commitments that are "ring-fenced" and insulated from typical operational pressures. This must be a strategic imperative to insulate the AI innovation capital.

The Fundamental Disconnect: POC Success vs. Production Paralysis

The journey from a demonstrated technical triumph in a lab environment to full production deployment is often fraught with difficulty. Analysis reveals a stark disconnect in the innovation pipeline: while significant potential for return on investment exists—with heavy AI investors reporting approximately 136% ROI over a three-year period—the scaling failure rate remains alarmingly high. Only 16% of AI projects successfully scale beyond the pilot phase, and only 25% yield positive returns.[1] This discrepancy is the core of the "AI paradox," where capital is deployed but fails to materialize as enterprise value because successful pilots cannot secure the consistent, large-scale funding needed for production deployment.

This failure often results not from technological shortcomings but from institutional paralysis driven by inconsistent funding—the "capitalization issues" cited in the transition phase. Operational budgets (OpEx) are inherently subject to quarterly volatility and short-term cost pressures. Funding complex, multi-quarter AI scaling initiatives through OpEx creates organizational uncertainty. When funding is unstable, technical teams often optimize for immediate *demo success* rather than *production resilience*, leading to accumulating technical debt, inefficient project management, and costly rework. This structural technical risk, induced by financial uncertainty, guarantees that promising initiatives lose momentum and fail the subsequent internal budget review required for scale-up.

The successful scaling and integration of AI necessitate a fundamental shift in organizational financial and strategic thinking. The dedicated AI POC funding mechanism must be administered and treated as internal Corporate Venture Capital (CVC). This model ensures that the capital is channeled specifically toward high-potential, growth-oriented initiatives that promise significant long-term value and competitive differentiation.

Scaling AI is not a matter of temporary projects; it is an exercise in building proprietary, strategic organizational assets. This requires significant investment in several durable components:

1. **Proprietary Model Development:** Creating unique, specialized AI models tailored to the organization's specific data, operational needs, and business objectives. These models form the core of the intellectual property.

2. **Robust Data Processing Pipelines:** Establishing durable, high-throughput, and scalable data infrastructure for the continuous ingestion, cleaning, transformation, and governance of the vast datasets required to train and maintain high-performing AI systems.

3. **Specialized, Durable Infrastructure:** Investing in dedicated, often GPU-intensive or customized computing infrastructure and platforms necessary to host, train, and run complex AI models efficiently at scale.

All these foundational elements—proprietary models, data pipelines, and specialized infrastructure—constitute enduring **capital expenditures (CapEx)**. They represent long-lived assets that increase the organization's overall productive capacity and strategic value.

Conversely, if these critical investments are mistakenly categorized and treated as transient **operational expenditures (OpEx)**, the organization fundamentally undermines its ability to build a sustainable AI capability. Treating them as OpEx leads to:

- **Inhibition of Durable Competitive Advantage:** Funds are focused on short-term fixes or external vendor services rather than building proprietary systems that cannot be easily replicated by competitors.

- **Prevention of Proprietary Intellectual Property (IP) Accrual:** The organization fails to create and retain unique, defensible IP assets in the form of custom models and data architecture.

- **Cyclical Inefficiency:** Continuous, non-accumulating spending on temporary solutions results in a lack of institutional knowledge, fragmented systems, and perpetually high recurring costs without an appreciating asset base.

Therefore, adopting a CapEx mentality is essential for the AI strategy. It frames AI development as an investment in future growth and market leadership, ensuring the organization accrues the durable assets and proprietary intellectual property necessary for sustained competitive advantage.

A dedicated budget, therefore, must be ring-fenced to strategically position the AI pipeline as a long-term investment. Data indicates that only 36% of organizations currently utilize dedicated AI innovation funds, while the majority rely on ad-hoc internal capital allocation (50%) or depend on cost savings generated by existing AI efficiencies (39%).[2] Establishing a dedicated fund is the strategic differentiator, ensuring that funds are consistently available for the transition phase rather than being diverted back into general operational needs.

The strategic allocation of a substantial, ring-fenced, and consistently available fund is not just a line item in a budget; it is the most unambiguous, measurable, and powerful demonstration of executive leadership's deep-seated commitment to rapid technological adaptation. This dedicated financial resource is the critical mechanism for "steering fast enough" to anticipate, integrate, and capitalize on emergent AI technologies, thereby sustaining a durable competitive advantage in a rapidly evolving market landscape.

Effective leadership alignment is a recognized, measurable differentiator that directly translates into superior business performance. This alignment necessitates C-suite consensus on the overarching AI strategy, including its ethical and operational frameworks, and requires the formal establishment of dedicated, cross-functional transformation structures (e.g., an AI Center of Excellence or Innovation Committee). Organizations that successfully cultivate this strong leadership consensus are shown to grow revenue at a rate up to 1.5 times faster than their peers and consistently realize a higher ROI from their AI initiatives. This demonstrates that strategic clarity and unified direction are as crucial as the technology itself.

The explicit financial commitment transcends mere verbal support; it acts as the essential catalyst for comprehensive organizational alignment. By providing this tangible funding, leadership signals to all crucial units, including technical, research, and business, that the AI transformation is an institutional priority backed by concrete capital, not simply a transient rhetorical objective. This mechanism operates analogously to large-scale philanthropic grants, where a significant, publicly declared financial backing is strategically employed to communicate serious intent and to drive measurable, profound, and sustained change across an organization or community.

Conversely, the absence of this structural financial backing leads to the inability to demonstrate a clear and predictable investment pipeline. This will inevitably cultivate internal skepticism. Without a concrete financial underpinning, doubts will rise across the enterprise regarding the longevity, strategic priority, and ultimate viability of AI initiatives. This skepticism becomes a corrosive force, significantly undermining enterprise-wide adoption, slowing down the pace of innovation, and ultimately jeopardizing the entire transformation effort. Therefore, the financial commitment is the organizational cornerstone, necessary to instill the confidence and stability required to integrate AI deeply and permanently into the business's core operations and culture.

The Financial Case: Justifying the Investment in an AI-Driven Future

To justify the necessary allocation of capital, the dedicated POC budget must be situated within the context of the massive global surge in AI investment and rigorously tied to measurable long-term value creation.

Global investment trends underscore the non-negotiable imperative of a robust, dedicated funding strategy. Corporate AI investment worldwide reached $252.3 billion in 2024, reflecting an expansion of more than thirteenfold over the past decade.[3] Competitive organizations must participate aggressively in this trajectory.

The acceleration of investment has been particularly acute in Generative AI (GenAI), which is the fastest-growing sector. Private investment in GenAI soared to $33.9 billion in 2024, representing an 18.7% increase from the previous year and exceeding 8.5 times the investment level seen in 2022.[3] This rapid expansion underscores that core innovative funding, especially for the POC pipeline, must be agile and highly liquid to respond to exponential technological shifts. With the U.S. widening its lead in global AI private investment (hitting $109.1 billion in 2024),[3] organizations lagging in establishing a funded pipeline risk falling into a significant competitive deficit.

The substantial influx of capital requires organizations to rigorously justify these investments by demonstrating a high potential for return on investment. Companies making significant AI investments report notable business advantages, including 82% higher revenue and 53% higher gross profit compared to non-adopters, translating to approximately 136% ROI over a three-year horizon.[1]

However, the "GenAI divide" persists, characterized by the fact that 95% of companies investing in AI show no meaningful ROI, and only 16% of projects successfully scale beyond the pilot phase.[1] This high failure rate in scaling proves that capital is being deployed, but it is not structured or governed effectively to manage the transition risk between pilot and production. The dedicated POC fund is specifically engineered to address this 84% scaling failure rate, acting as the structural bridge needed to transform high technical potential into realized revenue.

The AI Investment ROI Paradox: Potential vs. Reality

Metric	Leading AI Adopters (Heavy Investment)	Laggards / Non-Adopters (Minimal/Poor Investment)	Implication for Dedicated Funding
Revenue Growth Signal	82% higher revenue reported[1]	Significantly lower or negative growth	Dedicated budget must target projects with validated revenue impact metrics
Three-Year ROI Projection	~136% ($1.36 return per $1 invested)[1]	Minimal or negative return	Sustained, multi-year funding is necessary to capture full ROI potential
Projects Scaling Beyond Pilot	Only 16% successfully scale beyond pilot phase[1]	Minimal scaling capability	Dedicated CVC model is critical to bridge the funding gap to production
Companies Showing Meaningful ROI	5% (inverse of 95% showing no meaningful ROI)[1]	95% show no meaningful ROI	Requires rigorous, objective criteria (Pillar 4 KPIs) to ensure capital only progresses high-potential POCs

The substantial investment surge coupled with the general lack of immediate ROI for most companies suggests that the capital expenditure timeline for true AI transformation is significantly longer than typical corporate budgeting cycles. The dedicated fund must mitigate the pressure of short-term ROI demands by protecting a sustained, multi-year funding horizon necessary to achieve the reported 136% ROI.[1]

To ensure this significant capital commitment is effective and yields transformative results, the allocated fund must be strictly mandated to back only "high-coherence strategies." These strategies are defined by their explicit and rigorous link between overarching economic competitiveness objectives and the flexible, targeted application of innovation funding. This foundational principle necessitates a paradigm shift in how ROI is calculated and justified.

The ROI must be evaluated based on the criteria of long-term value creation, moving beyond the immediate and often limited scope of cost savings. Key metrics for success will include:

1. **Enhancing Business Operations:** Implementing AI and advanced technologies to create more efficient, resilient, and high-quality core business processes.

2. **Boosting Innovation Capability:** Investing in foundational research and development of new intellectual property, and establishing a culture that accelerates the time-to-market for novel solutions.

3. **Creating New Growth Opportunities:** Identifying, piloting, and scaling completely new product lines, service offerings, or market entries that fundamentally expand the organization's revenue streams and competitive footprint.

This is where the Innovation Committee comes in as a critical pillar. The IC has the responsibility for the execution of this vision. It requires the utilization of a rigorous CVC blueprint adapted for internal scaling projects. Successful scaling initiatives must focus intently on identifying and prioritizing specific, high-impact use cases that meet defined criteria:

- **Manual, Repetitive Tasks:** targeting processes characterized by high human intervention, subjectivity, and throughput volume, where automation can deliver immediate consistency and free up human capital for strategic work

- **High Data Volume/Velocity:** applying AI and machine learning to environments where the sheer scale and speed of data generation overwhelm traditional analytical methods, turning data overload into a source of competitive insight
- **Measurable Cost/Time Savings Potential:** requiring a clear, quantifiable business case that projects tangible reductions in OpEx or significant decreases in process cycle times

By adhering to this framework, the dedicated innovation funding is strategically directed toward value-driven outcomes, ensuring that every dollar invested contributes directly to the long-term, structural enhancement of the organization's competitive edge rather than being diffused across non-essential or low-impact projects. This structured approach is the linchpin for transforming capital commitment into sustained strategic advantage.

Strategic Reallocation from Mature Categories

Establishing a dedicated POC fund is fundamentally a zero-sum exercise that demands a purposeful reallocation of resources, signaling a commitment to future growth over the maintenance of legacy systems and the status quo.

IT leaders must make explicit choices to reallocate budgets, primarily by "squeezing mature categories" that offer diminishing returns. Many companies are reducing spending on traditional software areas, IT leaders are extending the useful life of hardware infrastructure from the typical 3 years for servers and 7 years for network equipment to at least 5 years for servers and 10 years for network equipment. This is essentially eliminating one refresh cycle.

The funds harvested from these established areas must then be prioritized for high-potential investments that drive strategic advantage. Top priorities include investments in advanced analytics and enhancing AI infrastructure along with widespread automation across not only IT but business workflows. This strategic divestment reinforces the cultural narrative that AI capabilities are the new foundational priority, accelerating organizational acceptance alongside financial commitment.

A major challenge confronting AI ROI is the poor allocation of existing capital. Research shows that nearly 70% of current AI budgets are allocated to areas that offer limited transformative value, often focusing on narrow applications, technical specifications, or generic tools that fail to align with core business needs.[4] This inefficiency is directly linked to the 95% failure rate in achieving meaningful ROI.[1]

The dedicated budget, governed by the CVC model, mandates a strategic assessment that eliminates spending on low-value tools. Instead, the focus must shift to strategic architecture, which offers long-term value and reshapes strategy. The dedicated fund ensures that capital targets high-impact, scalable business objectives, thereby resolving the pervasive misallocation issue upfront.

Adopting the Corporate Venture Capital Approach to Internal POCs

The inherent high-risk, high-reward profile of early-stage AI innovation necessitates a highly structured and disciplined approach to investment. The Corporate Venture Capital model provides the optimal internal framework for managing these characteristics, ensuring that capital deployment is both strategically aligned and financially responsible. It serves as the institutional mechanism for making rigorous, sophisticated investment decisions within the complex domain of emerging AI technologies.

The implementation of the CVC approach for the internal AI POC pipeline involves a crucial fusion of strict financial investment principles with core corporate capabilities. This framework actively combines:

- **Strict Financial Investment Principles:** maintaining the rigor of external venture capital, applying high standards for due diligence, projected return on investment, and measurable success criteria
- **Strategic Internal Partnerships:** fostering deep collaboration between technical innovation teams and core business units to ensure solutions address real, high-value corporate problems

- **Technology Co-innovation:** leveraging internal R&D capabilities and existing technology stacks to build prototypes that are readily compatible with the organization's infrastructure
- **Market Access Leveraging Subject Matter Expertise:** utilizing the company's deep industry knowledge and access to proprietary data and internal users to validate commercial viability and initial user acceptance

The internal CVC fund must maintain a disciplined and defined mandate, moving beyond speculative pure research. Its primary focus should be:

1. **Financing Pilot Projects and Proofs of Concept:** specifically targeting initiatives that are designed to solve clearly defined corporate problems with measurable business impact
2. **Supporting Successful Internal Innovations:** prioritizing and accelerating projects that have demonstrated initial promise and clear alignment with corporate strategy, rather than engaging in high-risk, unproven external ventures

To actively mitigate pure research and development risk, the fund's investment criteria should favor projects focusing on:

- **Functional Prototypes:** moving rapidly from conceptual design to tangible, working models
- **Market-Ready Internal Products:** ensuring the outcome is an internal tool or product that can be deployed and scaled within the organization quickly, thereby accelerating the time-to-value

This disciplined focus serves as a necessary check against investing purely based on technological "hype." It forces development teams to perform rigorous due diligence and articulate compelling, tangible business cases before capital is committed.

A successful internal CVC strategy mandates "high-coherence," which is the critical function of effectively bridging the organization's overarching **economic competitiveness objectives** with flexible yet accountable innovation funding instruments.

Investment decisions must be underpinned by a rigorous process of **use case identification and scoping**, utilizing a defined set of measurable criteria, including:

- **Measurable Cost/Time Savings Potential:** quantifiable metrics demonstrating the project's ROI through efficiency gains or expense reduction
- **High Data Volume Necessity:** validating that the AI solution requires the scale and specificity of the company's proprietary data to provide a competitive advantage
- **Regulatory and Compliance Feasibility:** early assessment of any legal, ethical, or compliance hurdles to ensure the solution is deployable in the real-world operational environment

The Innovation Committee (Pillar 3) serves as the organization's internal venture board. This empowered governance structure is responsible for establishing and rigorously monitoring clearly defined strategic checkpoints for every funded project.

This committee ensures a crucial oversight function: capital tranches are only released when there is confirmed strategic alignment and the project's continued viability has been validated against pre-defined success metrics. This centralized, empowered structure is critical for:

- **Overcoming Cross-Functional Friction:** providing a neutral, executive-level body to resolve resource and priority conflicts between different business units
- **Maintaining C-Suite Consensus:** ensuring continuous, shared understanding and support for the evolving, often complex, AI strategy
- **Mitigating Hidden Costs:** actively preventing the downstream financial losses associated with inefficient project management, unclear communication, and lack of accountability

Under the CVC model, capital is not released as a single, large lump sum. Instead, funding is deployed in contingent tranches. This staged investment approach is the primary mechanism for mitigating the inherent financial risk often associated with the large CapEx investments traditional in technology projects.

Tranching ensures that each POC progresses with a clear sense of purpose and accountability. The major benefit of this approach is immediate risk containment:

- **Strategic Failure Point:** If a project fails to meet a predefined strategic checkpoint—whether related to a shortfall in technical feasibility, insufficient data readiness, or poor initial user acceptance—the remaining capital tranches are **halted immediately**.
- **Financial Safeguard:** This mechanism saves the organization significant downstream investment that would otherwise be wasted on a non-viable venture, maximizing the efficiency of the innovation budget.

The release of subsequent tranches is strictly tied to the consistent achievement of measurable Key Performance Indicators (Pillar 4). These KPIs must provide objective evidence of the project's progress, business impact, and continued viability. Critically, these metrics must move beyond basic technical specifications to include: demonstrated potential for ROI, successful integration into existing workflows, and confirmed user adoption rates. This requirement systematically avoids the common pitfall of the 70% misallocation problem, where technical achievements are pursued without sufficient strategic business value. By quantifying progress into financial and operational metrics, the KPIs act as the essential common language between technical innovation teams and the finance committee, ensuring the viability of the project is translated into a defensible business case for the next round of funding.[4]

A dedicated POC budget is essential for strategic decision-making on AI scaling, enabling a conscious choice between CapEx and OpEx for final production. This flexibility is vital for balancing long-term asset value and cost efficiency.

However, OpEx models, such as SaaS, pose significant risks for mission-critical, proprietary AI systems:

1. **Long-Term Financial Inefficiency:** Recurring OpEx fees often lead to a **Total Cost of Ownership (TCO)** that surpasses an upfront CapEx investment within five years, compromising long-term cost goals.

2. **Vendor Volatility and Market Risk:** The rapid AI landscape makes relying on an OpEx vendor a gamble. Vendor failure or acquisition forces costly, disruptive migration.

3. **Loss of Control and Operational Dependency:** OpEx creates high **external dependency** on the provider's **Uptime/SLAs**, service quality, and pricing structure. This vulnerability to price hikes and **vendor lock-in** poses a major operational risk.

4. **Compromising Competitive Advantage:** Adopting OpEx for strategic proprietary AI **outsources a potential competitive advantage**. CapEx, by contrast, allows the organization to build, own, and fully govern core AI assets as an enduring source of internal value.

The dedicated POC fund, positioned as strategic capital, enables the organization to secure asset ownership and maximize long-term ROI. CapEx requires high upfront investment but mitigates the financial strain of this initial cost. CapEx provides asset ownership, potentially lower cumulative costs over the long term, and greater internal control over maintenance and data.

The inherent risk of obsolescence (purchased software quickly becoming outdated) associated with CapEx is mitigated by embedding mandatory, regular updates, maintenance budgeting, and technical gate reviews directly into the CVC governance checkpoints (Pillars 3 & 4).

Comparative Risk Analysis:
Funding AI Scaling (CapEx vs. OpEx Model)

Risk Factor	Dedicated CapEx (Dedicated POC Fund)	Operational OpEx/SaaS (Volatile Funding)	Mitigation Strategy via CVC Framework
Upfront Financial Strain	High initial outlay, significant financial risk	Low initial cost, spread over time	Implement strategic tranches contingent on ROI checkpoints (Pillar 4)
Obsolescence / Security	Risk of outdated software without regular updates	Continuous updates inherent in subscription	Require mandatory technical gate review and scheduled capital updates during tranching
Long-Term Cost	Lower cumulative cost over 5+ years, asset ownership	Higher cumulative cost due to recurring fees	Dedicated fund must prioritize proprietary IP and scalable infrastructure for multi-year viability analysis
Reliability and Dependency	High internal control, greater autonomy	Contingent on provider uptime and service quality	Establish stringent Service Level Agreements (SLAs) or prioritize in-house deployment where strategic
Budget Volatility	Insulated from quarterly pressures (ring-fenced)	Subject to short-term cost-cutting demands	The dedicated fund provides stability, preventing momentum loss due to capitalization issues

Recommendations for Financial and IT Leaders

The success of launching AI projects into production is inextricably linked to the adoption of a dedicated, governed funding mechanism. By implementing a CVC approach for internal POCs, organizations can manage risk, ensure strategic alignment, and convert technological potential into durable competitive advantage.

The dedicated budget must be structured as a perpetual, revolving CVC fund. Successful, scaled projects should transition their operational costs out of the initial POC fund and into standard OpEx or dedicated CapEx amortization schedules. Crucially, the ROI generated by these successful ventures should be systematically tracked and reinvested back into the dedicated fund, creating a self-sustaining loop that continually fuels new innovation. To maintain strategic coherence, the Innovation Committee (Pillar 3) and the Chief Financial Officer (CFO) must conduct an annual review to reassess strategic allocation and realign the dedicated budget with the organization's highest-level growth objectives.

The establishment of a successful AI production pipeline requires four primary actionable steps in financial governance:

1. **Ring-Fence the Capital:** Immediately establish a separate, non-OpEx budget line item dedicated solely to the AI POC pipeline, formally defining it as internal Corporate Venture Capital to insulate it from operational volatility.

2. **Mandate Strategic Harvest:** Implement policies that mandate strategic reallocation, diverting capital from the 70% of misallocated AI spending and reducing non-essential expenditure in mature IT categories to fund the pipeline.

3. **Institutionalize Governance:** Formalize the Innovation Committee (Pillar 3) and mandate the use of staged funding tranches tied explicitly to measurable Key Performance Indicators (Pillar 4), ensuring accountability and strategic coherence throughout the scaling process.

4. **Prioritize Ownership:** For high-value, strategic POCs, ensure the final funding tranches are sufficient to secure proprietary CapEx ownership. This maximizes long-term ROI and competitive advantage, preventing the organization from defaulting to long-term OpEx dependency for core assets.

The dedicated budget serves as the organization's most effective risk management tool. It mitigates financial risk by linking investment directly to performance checkpoints and manages strategic risk by guaranteeing that market-ready innovations are not lost to bureaucratic delays. By institutionalizing this disciplined CVC framework, organizations transform the risk profile of AI innovation from high, unstructured, and unpredictable to managed, measured, and strategically aligned.

CHAPTER 7

The Production Mandate:
Operationalizing the Five Pillars for Enterprise AI Success

The ultimate pinnacle of the AI Production Pyramid is **Production**. This is the state where AI is seamlessly woven into the enterprise fabric, delivering sustained, measurable financial and operational value.

The transition from a nascent artificial intelligence Proof of Concept to a fully integrated, scalable, and trustworthy production system represents the singular, defining challenge of the current cognitive industrial revolution. This playbook began by foregrounding the critical AI Paradox: despite unprecedented global investment and the immense promise of AI—projected to contribute trillions to global productivity—a staggering 80% of AI projects fail to successfully move beyond the experimental pilot phase. This widespread failure is rarely a technical or algorithmic deficiency; rather, it is a deep-seated business and structural deficit. It is driven by intermittent and inconsistent funding models, a critical lack of senior, cross-functional strategic direction, and, most fundamentally, insufficient organizational readiness to absorb and govern this new technology.

The definitive solution to bridging this devastating "pilot-to-production" chasm is not found in pursuing marginal algorithmic improvements but in establishing superior organizational governance, fostering a mature, AI-centric culture, and architecting a stable financial foundation. The success of the enterprise-wide AI production mandate rests entirely upon the institutionalization and operational excellence of the **Five Operational Pillars**. These pillars are the essential structural scaffolding—the non-negotiable architecture—required to convert technical feasibility (a successful POC) into enterprise-grade trust, compliance, risk mitigation, and the sustained, measurable delivery of business value (Production). By deeply embedding these five pillars, organizations can systematically de-risk their entire AI portfolio, radically accelerate their time-to-value, and ensure that every dollar invested in AI translates directly into a durable, quantifiable competitive advantage.

These five pillars must be conceptualized and managed as concurrent maturity journeys rather than as a sequential checklist of one-time checkpoints. Their simultaneous progression forms the robust foundation for a resilient, AI-augmented enterprise:

1. **Data Readiness:** This pillar encompasses establishing a centralized, high-quality data governance framework; ensuring data lineage, security, and accessibility; and instituting continuous monitoring for data drift and quality degradation—the lifeblood of any production AI system.

2. **Workforce Education and Skills Transformation:** This addresses the critical need to upskill and reskill the existing workforce, not just in data science but across legal, operations, finance, and leadership. It involves creating a common AI literacy and fostering the human-machine collaboration required to manage automated processes.

3. **Innovation Committee and Portfolio Management:** This pillar mandates the establishment of a senior-level, cross-functional committee responsible for prioritizing AI use cases based on strategic alignment and quantifiable ROI, managing the portfolio of active POCs, and ensuring consistent resource allocation.

4. **Strategic Alignment and Business Integration:** AI systems must solve high-value, enterprise-level problems. This pillar ensures that every AI project is directly aligned with the top-tier corporate strategy, has a clear operational owner, and is integrated seamlessly into existing business processes and decision-making workflows.

5. **Dedicated POC Funding and Financial Architecture:** Moving beyond ad-hoc, siloed IT budgets, this requires establishing a dedicated, risk-tolerant venture-style fund for Proofs of Concept,

with clear transition criteria and a predictable, multi-year funding pathway to scale successful pilots.

The ultimate achievement, the apex of the entire AI Production Pyramid, is **Production**. This is defined as the operational state where AI systems are no longer projects but are seamlessly and invisibly woven into the enterprise fabric, operating reliably, compliantly, and autonomously to deliver continuous, sustained, and measurable financial and operational value back to the organization.

The journey is systematic, managed through the phases outlined in the AI Data Readiness Roadmap:

- **POC (4–8 weeks):** focus on technical feasibility, defining the Minimal Viable Dataset (MVD), and **integrating compliance** requirements (Pillar 1 & 3)
- **Pilot (8–12 weeks):** focus on business viability, demonstrating measurable ROI on the use case (Pillar 4), implementing initial **targeted training for core users** (Pillar 2), and justifying the first dedicated funding tranche (Pillar 5)
- **Scale to Production (6–12 months):** focus on enterprise readiness, building the connected data fabric, establishing continuous governance (Pillar 3), and releasing final funding based on KPI adherence (Pillar 5)

The successful organization understands that this is not a one-time project but a new, managed discipline. By institutionalizing the Five Operational Pillars, leadership transforms the high, unstructured, and unpredictable risk profile of AI innovation into a managed, measured, and strategically aligned engine for future growth. The mandate is clear: Governance and strategic architecture must be the accelerator, not the impediment, to innovation. Only then can the organization transcend the AI Paradox and realize the full, transformative potential of its investments.

The time for experimentation is over. The era of enterprise AI production begins now.

Author Bio

Dorren Schmitt, PhD, is a transformative technology leader and innovator with over 30 years of experience. At The Weather Channel and Allen Media Group, she has spent more than two decades spearheading engineering initiatives, including artificial intelligence, high-performance computing, virtualization, enterprise applications, enterprise infrastructure modernization, data and cloud migration, M&A integration, cybersecurity, and digital transformation. She architected and now leads the teams responsible for end-user, enterprise, and security infrastructure across hybrid cloud environments, as well as the enterprise-wide AI and IT strategy. Dorren is currently driving the modernization of legacy systems through innovative AI and cloud solutions and defining the future of the company's digital transformation. Each of these initiatives has been transformational for The Weather Channel in staying the "Most Trusted News Network."

Before joining The Weather Channel, she taught mathematics at the University of New Orleans. A dedicated community leader, she has served on numerous non-profit boards, including the Technology Association of GA (TAG), TAG ED, and Gwinnett Technical College. She passionately mentors young women pursuing STEM careers and is a sought-after speaker at industry conferences on topics such as digital transformation, AI, and building high-performing teams.

Dorren holds a B.S. in Mathematics and Secondary Education, an M.Ed. in Curriculum and Instruction, an M.A. in Applied Statistics, and a PhD in Applied Statistics. Her accomplishments have been recognized with prestigious awards, including The Weather Company Leadership Award (2013), multiple nominations for The Weather Channel Storm Award, Woman of the Year for Women in Technology (2019), and Top 50 Women Leaders in Atlanta (2025).

Dorren is available for speaking engagements and consulting with organizations seeking to implement AI. She can be reached on LinkedIn at https://www.linkedin.com/in/dorren-schmitt-ph-d/ and at DrDorrenAI@Gmail.com. Any feedback on this book would be greatly appreciated, as would reviews added to the book page on Amazon.

Appendix

Chapter 1

1. Hannah Mayer, Lareina Yee, Michael Chui, and Roger Roberts, "AI in the workplace: A report for 2025," McKinsey, (2025) https://www.mckinsey.com/capabilities/mckinsey-digital/our-insights/superagency-in-the-workplace-empowering-people-to-unlock-ais-full-potential-at-work

Chapter 3

1. Sharpen Admin, "How Netflix Faced A Digital Transformation: A Case Study," Sharpen Technologies, https://sharpencx.com/netflix-digital-transformation-case-study/

2. Chandan Mishra, "Data Analytics Case Studies & Examples for Various Industries," ScikIQ (2023) https://scikiq.com/blog/data-analytics-case-studies-that-will-inspire-you/

Chapter 4

1. Fiona Briggs, "IBM report: two-thirds of UK firms gain from AI—reskilling key to unlocking greater productivity," (2025) https://retailtimes.co.uk/ibm-report-two-thirds-of-uk-firms-gain-from-ai-reskilling-key-to-unlocking-greater-productivity/

2. Ling Huang and Yuping Zhao, "The impact of AI literacy on work–life balance and job satisfaction among university faculty," (2025) https://pmc.ncbi.nlm.nih.gov/articles/PMC12487956/

3. Chris, "5 Steps to Build AI Training for Non-Tech Teams," (2025) https://blog.naitive.cloud/5-steps-to-build-ai-training-for-non-tech-teams/

4. Matt Kelly, "AI Literacy Training: A Compliance Necessity Under the EU AI Act," (2025) https://www.navex.com/en-us/blog/article/ai-literacy-training-a-compliance-necessity-under-the-eu-ai-act/

5. Mark Hudson, "AI Ethics and Responsible Use," Traliant, (2026) https://www.traliant.com/courses/ai-ethics-responsible-use/

6. Data Society, "Measuring the ROI of AI and Data Training: A Productivity-First Approach," (2025) https://datasociety.com/measuring-the-roi-of-ai-and-data-training-a-productivity-first-approach/

Chapter 5

1. Dilip Mohapatra, "The Role of MLOps in AI Governance & Compliance," (2025) https://blog.cognitiveview.com/the-role-of-mlops-in-ai-governance-and-compliance/

Chapter 6

1. The Data Experts, "The ROI of AI Investments: Are Current Expenditures Justified?" Insights, (2025) https://thedataexperts.us/insights/ai-investment-roi-analysis-2025

2. Eugene Khvostov, "The complex costs of AI: Investments, funding and ROI tracking," CFO Dive, (2025) https://www.cfodive.com/spons/the-complex-costs-of-ai-investments-funding-and-roi-tracking/761245/

3. Njenga Kariuki, "Economy | The 2025 AI Index Report," Stanford HAI, (2025) https://hai.stanford.edu/ai-index/2025-ai-index-report/economy

4. Dimitris Dimitriadis, "The Truth About AI Budgets: Why 70% Goes to the Wrong Places," TheFutureCats, (2025) https://thefuturecats.com/the-truth-about-ai-budgets-why-70-goes-to-the-wrong-places/

www.ingramcontent.com/pod-product-compliance
Lightning Source LLC
Chambersburg PA
CBHW052355060726
47592CB00020B/2447